Moon Phases

Moon Phases
A Symbolic Key

Martin Goldsmith

1469 Morstein Road
West Chester, Pennsylvania 19380 USA

International Standard Book Number: 0-914918-83-4
Library of Congress Catalog Card Number: 88-50421

Published by Whitford Press
a division of Schiffer Publishing Ltd.
1469 Morstein Road
West Chester, Pennsylvania 19380

Manufactured in the United States of America

This book may be purchased from the publisher.
Please include $2.00 postage
Try your bookstore first.

About the Author

Martin Goldsmith has been an avid astrologer for twenty years. His areas of special interest are Sabian symbols, Egyptian astrology, and, of course, the Moon Phases. He is currently enrolled in a Ph.D. program in European history, and spends what little time remains to him in researching astrology and in gardening. His next book will be on the sign Aquarius.

Other Astrology books from Whitford Press

Astrology & Relationships, by Mary Devlin
Planets in Signs, by Skye Alexander
**Planets in Love: Exploring Your Emotional
  and Sexual Needs,** by John Townley
**Planets in Aspect: Understanding Your Inner
  Dynamics,** by Robert Pelletier
**Planets in Houses: Experiencing Your
  Environment,** by Robert Pelletier
**Planets in Composite: Analyzing Human
  Relationships,** by Robert Hand
**Planets in Transit: Life Cycles for
  Living,** by Robert Hand
Planets in Youth: Patterns of Early Development,
  by Robert Hand
Astrology & Past Lives, by Mary Devlin
Compendium of Astrology, by Rose
  Lineman and Jan Popelka
Birth Pattern Psychology, by Tamise Van Pelt
Astrology, Nutrition and Health, by Robert
  Carl Jansky
Essays on Astrology, by Robert Hand
Horoscope Symbols, by Robert Hand
Astrology Inside Out, by Bruce Nevin
**World Ephemeris: 20th Century, Midnight
  Edition,** by Para Research
World Ephemeris: 20th Century, Noon Edition,
  by Para Research

Acknowledgments

Special thanks to my brother, Ken, for providing the thousands of birth dates used in my research.

Thanks also to Rick Klimczak and Dale O'Brien, whose ideas form the basis of the energy flow theory and the lunar subphase theory.

Contents

1. Historical Background and Research Methods 13

2. Sun, Moon, and Moon Phase 25

3. How to Find Your Moon Phase 49

4. Phase 1: The Lily Pond 59

5. Phase 2: The Trickster 63

6. Phase 3: The New World 67

7. Phase 4: The Warrior Princess 71

8. Phase 5: The Romantic 75

9. Phase 6: The Rebel 79

10. Phase 7: The Plowman 83

11. Phase 8: The Actress 87

12. Phase 9: The Gathering of Friends 91

13. Phase 10: The Architect 95

14. Phase 11: The Dream Wedding **99**

15. Phase 12: The Warrior King **103**

16. Phase 13: The Dancer **109**

17. Phase 14: The Vision Quest **113**

18. Phase 15: The Beloved **117**

19. Phase 16: The Procession...........................**121**

20. Phase 17: The Conjuror **127**

21. Phase 18: The Angel **131**

22. Phase 19: The Wise Serpent **135**

23. Phase 20: The Forgiven Heart **139**

24. Phase 21: The Besieged Church.....................**145**

25. Phase 22: The Carnival.............................**149**

26. Phase 23: The Widowed Queen **153**

27. Phase 24: The Magic Realm **157**

28. Phase 25: The Great Teacher **163**

29. Phase 26: The Pied Piper **167**

30. Phase 27: The Saint **173**

31. Phase 28: The Prophet **177**

32. The System **181**

33. Energy Flow in the Individual Chart **205**

34. Epilogue: Towards a Lunar Astrology **229**

Bibliography and Recommended Reading **235**

Into the Twilight

Out-worn heart, in a time out-worn,
Come clear of the nets of wrong and right;
Laugh, heart, again in the grey twilight,
Sigh, heart, again in the dew of the morn.

Your mother Eire is always young,
Dew ever shining and twilight grey;
Though hope fall from you and love decay,
Burning in fires of a slanderous tongue.

Come, heart, where hill is heaped upon hill:
For there the mystical brotherhood
Of sun and moon and hollow and wood
And river and stream work out their will;

And God stands winding His lonely horn,
And time and the world are ever in flight;
And love is less kind than the grey twilight,
And hope is less dear than the dew of the morn.

William Butler Yeats

Chapter One

Historical Background and Research Methods

In 1917, four days after his marriage, William Butler Yeats began receiving strange teachings from a consciousness beyond the grave. His wife served as the channel, delivering the messages first through automatic writing, and later by talking in her sleep. During the next seven years Yeats pieced together the notes and scribblings that he and his wife had gathered. The outcome of this research was a book called *A Vision*[1] which outlined an elaborate metaphysical system relating variations of the human personality to the phases of the Moon. The book wasn't exactly astrology, since it provided no system by which to assign an individual's Moon phase. Yeats had selected examples for the phases entirely by intuition, and hadn't even considered which phase of the Moon these people were born under. This oversight is puzzling, considering Yeats' familiarity with astrology. Perhaps he was just following the advice of his spirit guides, who had specifically told him that the material was to be used in his poetry. Unfortunately, by straddling the occult and literary fields, Yeats ended up losing both audiences.

The problem was not so much Yeats' as the world's. Since Yeats himself was a synthetic thinker he overlooked the fact that astrology and literature, at least in modern times, have become hopelessly compartmentalized. So while astrologers looked for simple formulas and resented Yeats' obscure poetics, the literary world was equally intolerant of Yeats' occultism. Unwilling to admit that Yeats' system might actually work, they approached *A Vision* as a literary curiosity, whose intellectual roots ran to obsolete astrological and Platonic doctrines.

In its prejudice against occultism, the literary world shamelessly downplayed the broad influence of occultism on Yeats' work, despite the fact that Yeats himself was constantly pointing it out. The following statement is hardly ambiguous:

> "If I had not made magic my constant study I could not have written a single word of my Blake book, nor would *The Countess Kathleen* have ever come to exist. The mystical life is the centre of all that I do and all that I think and all that I write. It holds to my work the same relation that the philosophy of Godwin held to the work of Shelley..."[2]

Poetry and Magic

While the literary community was at work fortifying its ivory tower, historian Frances Yates had begun to undermine the entire structure through her discovery of Neoplatonic influences in the works of Spenser, Shakespeare, and Milton.[3] Similar connections had been made before, but never by someone of Ms. Yates' caliber. As an historian, Frances Yates was rigorous and thorough. Thus her research, rather than falling into the dustbin traditionally reserved for offbeat subjects, has become the starting point for many scholarly inquiries into the Hermetic and occult tradition.

It has long been known that Elizabethan England was heavily influenced by the Italian Renaissance, and had adopted much of its Neoplatonic philosophy. It is no surprise, then, to find Renaissance occultism in the poetry of the Elizabethan Age. But what Frances Yates was finding was a conscious championing of these ideas-even after they had lost their popularity. Because of her scruples as an historian, Yates drew few conclusions from these findings. However, it's easy enough to see the connections.

Both occultism and poetry rely on the power of symbols. Through symbols they attempt to evoke emotions and to communicate supra-rational knowledge. Poets have a natural attraction to magic because magic involves the conscious manipulation of symbols. And magic doesn't just play around with images for superficial effect; it looks for symbols with power, symbols which are connected with the energy of the Universal Mind, or in Jung's terms, the Collective Unconscious. The magical tradition may not share the same vocabulary as Jungian psychology, but it has always known of the archetypes and their powers, and has even spent a great deal of time cataloguing them. The tarot is one such catalogue; the Cabala, another.

Now it would obviously be false to say that all poets are occultists, but the fact remains that many of the world's best poets have been versed in the occult arts. These poets have fulfilled the ancient role of the shaman or medicine man, who was at once a poet, a magician, a lawmaker, and a theologian. Frances Yates has shown that Spenser, Shakespeare, and Milton consciously developed an occult substrata to their work. [4] To these names one may add the even more obvious examples of Dante, Blake, and Yeats. All of these poets were working with moral and theological themes, and their poetry, though strong on natural imagery, is also charged with the supernatural. Since Yeats was a practicing magician as well as a poet, he had a particularly deep understanding of these matters. Anticipating the ideas of Jung, he spoke of a "racial memory," which could be accessed through deep introspection. He believed that the keys to this palace of memory were symbols, and that these symbolic keys could be used to explain the simple magic of primitive peoples:

"Such magical simples as the husk of the flax, water out of the fork of an elm-tree, do their work as I think, by awaking in the depths of the mind where it mingles with the Great Mind, and is enlarged by the Great Memory, some creative energy, some hypnoticc command. They are not what we call faith cures, for they have been much used and successfully, the traditions of all lands affirm, over children and over animals..."[5]

In other words, symbols give access to memories, which are composed not only of ideas and information, but also of energy and power.

Like shamans, poets are close observers of nature. Poets are able to see in nature the hidden forms of the archetypes, and thus are able to extract from their environment—from the trees, animals, clouds, and people—many hidden messages. By putting these archetypal images into artistic form, they can share these insights with others, and help them rediscover their own well-springs of natural wisdom.

Yeats' Golden Dawn

Apart from the Theosophical Society, the Golden Dawn was probably the most important magical society of the last two centuries. The Golden Dawn was the more radical of the organizations, for despite its Rosicrucian origins, it was the spiritual heir of Freemasonry, from which it borrowed its emphasis on ritual magic, grades, and initiations. The Golden Dawn had its share of scandal, and the literary community was only too happy to capitalize on it, representing Yeats' membership as a misguided foible, or a feather in the cap of an otherwise disreputable organization. This was a complete misrepresentation; Yeats was an important leader of the organization from its very inception.

The occult revival in England was an importation from France, generated largely through the occult novels of Edward Bulwer-Lytton, who was a disciple of the French magician Eliphas Levi. The decadent romanticism of the English revival—the robes and spells, séances and secret texts—can thus be seen as a product of the literary imagination of the late nineteenth century. Bulwer-Lytton was immensely popular in his time, but he was actually a dreadful writer. In fact there is now a Bulwer-Lytton literary contest devoted to the creation of the worst possible opening line for a novel.

The Golden Dawn was an outgrowth of a study group called the Hermetic Society, of which Yeats was also a member. When the founder of the Hermetic Society died in 1888, two of its more prominent members, Wynn Westcott and McGregor Mathers, founded the Golden Dawn. As the more confident and creative of the two, Mathers composed all of the society's original rituals. Unfortunately, within a short time he had assumed a dictatorial pre-eminence within the organization. There were plenty of grumblings, but for the time being Mathers kept a lid on the situation. However, when he moved to Paris and started promoting Egyptian rites—in a public theater no less—revolt broke out in earnest. There were several reasons for the London Lodge's break with Mathers, but a major factor was its refusal to recognize Mathers' recent initiation of Aleister Crowley.[6] On this score Yeats was adamant, declaring that the Golden Dawn was not a reformatory[7], and speaking of Crowley as "a person of unspeakable life."[8] Crowley richly deserved this epithet. Already well on his way to becoming the world's most notorious black magician, he was later to call himself "The Beast" and file his teeth into points. And while his amusing theatrics have often thrown people off the scent, Crowley was a truly evil man—a man of great natural power who had a disastrous effect on the lives of those who surrounded him. It was inevitable that Yeats and Crowley would clash—the white magician and the black.

In April of 1900, Mathers sent Aleister Crowley to take over the London Lodge and expel half its membership for insubordination. Breaking into the Lodge's meeting rooms, he seized the property on Mathers' behalf, but was quickly expelled when an irate member called a constable. When Yeats found out what was going on, he changed the locks and took up residence in the rooms, hoping to confront Crowley on his return. He was not disappointed. Crowley showed up two nights later, wearing a highland kilt, a black mask, a dagger, and a huge crucifix.[9] It seems that Crowley's latest kick was dressing up in costumes and taking on assumed identities.

Yeats blocked Crowley at the door, and Crowley retreated to get a constable. Not surprisingly, the police sided with Yeats (Who's going to trust a masked man in a kilt?). This incident was the last straw. Mathers and Crowley were expelled from the Golden Dawn, and Yeats emerged, more or less by default,[10] as its new spiritual leader.

But more trouble was ahead. Yeats and the Lodge's secretary were soon isolated as the Society's new authoritarians. Yeats, it seems, wanted to maintain the organization's hierarchical structure, with its grades and examinations, while most of the other members wanted something more informal. Many of them were already involved in a titillating séance scene—and were taking their guidance from an Egyptian spirit residing in a statue in the British Museum. Yeats felt that this was mere dabbling. As one of the most religious members of the group, he was always mindful of the society's real goal: mystical union with God. He also wanted to maintain the Christian identity of the group, which had been founded as a Rosicrucian society, and was therefore deeply involved in the symbolic and mystical aspects of Christianity. This conflict between Christian mysticism and Egyptian magic was never fully resolved; most of the members were pulled in one direction or the other.[11]

In 1903, Arthur Waite was elected president of the society (now called the Morgenrothe). When he moved to abolish examinations, eliminate all magical work, and turn the society into a study group for his own brand of Christian mysticism, it was Yeats who opposed him. And when this revolt failed, Yeats split from the society and formed the *Stella Matutina,* with the majority of the membership in tow. Yeats was to remain active in this organization until the last years of his life.

The chronic instability of the Golden Dawn was inevitable given its internal structure. Setting up an authoritarian, theocratic organization in the midst of a modern democracy just wasn't a very good idea. With no legitimized method for delegating and transferring power, the society soon became a free-for-all for spiritual power-trippers, where anybody could clamber to the top and then solidify his or her position by claiming authority from "Hidden Masters." This same problem has plagued the Theosophical Society, and many other spiritual organizations.

When the Golden Dawn was formed, the wisdom tradition of the East had just been rediscovered, and the issues of discipleship vs. personal will had not been unraveled. Yeats himself proved inconsistent on these issues. Thus while he avoided the Theosophical Society because of its emphasis on hidden masters, he promoted a similar hierarchy within the Golden Dawn. His motives for this were probably pure; his idealism may have simply blinded him to the reality of human power lust.

The Golden Dawn certainly had its problems, but it was nonetheless a creative and influential cultural force. In scholarship and intelligence it easily surpassed the occult dabblings of the Renaissance. Dion Fortune's book on the Cabala, for instance, is probably the best book on the Cabala ever written. The Golden Dawn's strong suit, however, was the tarot. Many of the decks available today—and almost all of the good ones—came out of the Golden Dawn. As I will attempt to show later on, Yeats' Moon phases emerged from the same matrix of thought; they were, in fact, a new and hidden form of the tarot.

While *A Vision* was not formally related to Yeats' work within the Golden Dawn, the connection is still pretty obvious. The exercises in meditation and visualization that Yeats was practicing would have made this type of channeling much easier. And though his wife was the channel, at least on a mechanical level, the material itself tells us that it was really Yeats' consciousness that was being channeled. In fact, the date of the first channeling—

October 24, 1917—shows Uranus making an exact transit over Yeats' Aquarian Moon.

On its publication in 1926, *A Vision* was greeted by a wall of silence. Yeats took this in stride. Much of his work was already beyond the comprehension of his audience, and he consoled himself with the thought that the book's impact lay somewhere in the distant future:

> *"A Vision* reminds me of the stones I used to drop as a child into a certain very deep well. The splash is very far off and very faint. Not a review except one by AE—either the publisher has sold the review copies or the editors have—and no response of any kind except from a very learned doctor in the North of England who sends me profound and curious extracts from ancient philosophies on the subject of gyres."[12]

Solar and Lunar Divisions

Yeats did not live to hear the first splash, which came a full fifty years later with the publication, in 1976, of *Phases of the Moon*, by Dorothy Wergin, Marilyn Busteed, and Richard Tiffany. *Phases of the Moon* resurrected Yeats' system by bringing it[13] into a more active relationship to the living. As a book written specifically for astrologers, *Phases of the Moon* immediately took up the problem of assigning individual Moon phases to specific portions of the lunar cycle. Simple as this may seem, it was a real breakthrough. For without a method by which to assign Moon phases, the system could never by anything but a castle in the air— a speculative theory with no grounding in reality. Even if several different methods of division were proposed, at least they could be tested with concrete examples. At least there would be something to work with.

Since Yeats' system has twenty-eight phases, with no indication that any one phase is more important than any other, the most obvious method of division would be twenty-eight equal phases of 12.86 degrees each. The authors of *Phases of the Moon*, however, also developed a more complex system, which they termed the "solar" system of division. It contains twenty-four small phases of 10 degrees each, and four large phases of 30 degrees each. (See Figures 3.1 and 3.2) I have known a few astrologers who use both the "solar" and "lunar" systems of division, claiming that there are only minor variations between the two. This, however, is impossible. Some of the phases in the "lunar" system don't even overlap with the analogous phases in the "solar" system. For instance, in the "solar" system Phase 2 extends from 30 degrees past the new Moon point to 40 degrees past the new Moon point (see Figure 3.1). In the "lunar" system Phase 2 extends from 13 degrees past the new Moon to 26 degrees past the new Moon. These arcs don't even overlap. So if the description for Phase 2 fits individuals born in both periods, it is obvious that either the description is very vague, or the Moon phases themselves are not particularly discrete.

In order to make an educated judgment on this controversy, I turned to my brother's data bank, which includes birth dates for thousands of famous people. Approximating the angle between the Sun and Moon, I arranged these examples in "solar" and "lunar" phases, looking in particular to those areas around the expanded solar phases, since these are the areas of greatest discrepancy. The results of my study strongly supported the "solar" system of division. Expanded Phases 8 and 22, in particular, seemed homogeneous. The other two expanded phases showed some differentiation, but not of the sort that would justify the creation of new phases. The system itself, meanwhile, worked so well, that I became an immediate fanatic; I continued my research, dividing the phases according to the "solar" system of division.

Putting aside the phase interpretations that I'd already read, I tried to get my first impressions directly from the examples. This wasn't hard; the qualities of the phases practically leapt from the page. I condensed my first scattered notes into short phase descriptions, which I revised and enlarged as my understanding of the phases grew. Several years later I was working with at least 10,000 sample charts. Beyond that I had discovered several other ways to access the Moon phases.

Perhaps the most exciting discovery presented in *Phases of the Moon* is the correlation between the Moon phases and the signs of the zodiac. This relationship is so solid that it would be no exaggeration to compare it to the age-old correspondence between the zodiacal signs and the astrological houses. As every astrologer knows, zodiacal correspondences form the basis of most house interpretations. When we talk about the fourth house, the "house of the home," we are aware that it is associated with the sign Cancer, and with the Moon, which is the ruler of Cancer. Wergin and Busteed discovered similar zodiacal and planetary correlations for the Moon phases. This was very helpful, for the Moon phases are such a new quantity that it is easy to get lost without some familiar guideposts. Yeats' terminology is certainly no help. Try telling astrologers that the Body of Fate for Phase 23 is found in Phase 21 and they won't even know what you are talking about. But tell them that Phase 23 is a Capricorn phase, ruled by Saturn, and it will mean a great deal.

It didn't take long to convince me of the zodiacal correspondences of the phases. In case after case the sign of the Moon phase was completely self-evident in the character of the examples, and even in their physical appearance. This was true even when there was no particular emphasis on that sign in the person's chart. The sign of the Moon phase usually is re-emphasized, but that's to be expected; important influences in the chart are often doubled or trebled. On the other hand, it would be foolish to say that the Moon phase only confirms what can be gathered from other areas of the chart.

On a simple astronomical level the Moon phase is the most obvious phenomena in the sky; it follows, then, that its effect on the personality should be equally obvious. It is my experience that the Moon phase is no less important than the Moon sign, and is almost as important as the Sun sign. This should come as no surprise. The lunar cycle is no less basic than the solar cycle and the circling of the seasons. The real cause for wonder, in fact, is that the Moon phases have been ignored for so long.

One of the most attractive features of the "solar" system of division—besides, of course, the fact that it works—is its emphasis on the zodiacal nature of the phases. The larger phases are 30 degrees wide—exactly the length of a zodiacal sign. And the smaller phases are 10 degrees wide, dividing each of the remaining signs into three equal parts.

Now the division of signs into three parts is a very old and revered astrological practice. According to the theory of *decanates*, the first 10 degrees of a zodiacal sign are ruled by the traditional ruler of the sign. For instance, the first decanate of Cancer is ruled by the Moon. The second 10 degrees of the sign are ruled by the planet that rules the next zodiacal sign of the same element. Since Cancer is a water sign, we would look to the next water sign, which is Scorpio, and then find its ruler. The ruler of Scorpio is Pluto, so the second decanate of Cancer should be ruled by Pluto. To find the ruler of the third decanate of Cancer we look to the ruler of Pisces, the remaining water sign. Neptune is the ruler of Pisces, so Neptune is the ruler of the third decanate of Cancer.

Personally, I have never held much with the idea of rulerships. For one thing, they keep changing. When Uranus was discovered, everyone thought it was a good idea to change the rulership of Aquarius from Saturn to Uranus. But recently a lot of people are starting to have second thoughts. At this point there are questions about the rulerships of Virgo, Libra, Scorpio, Aquarius, and Pisces. That's practically half the signs! Considering how much stock traditional astrologers place in rulerships, it is obvious that astrology is really changing. And I'm all for it, for what we're seeing is the demise of a very formulaic and judgmental type of astrology, stressing rulers, exaltations, falls, and detriments. In the new astrology relationships between the signs and planets are more fluid. This ruins all our neat little systems; it ruins the type of astrology that rattles off rulers and detriments like beads on an abacus. Astrologers today have to actually think about the combinations; they have to consider how the energies might work together, and not simply whether they are "good" or "bad."

If the rulers of the signs are not particularly trustworthy, then how can we possibly trust the rulers of the decanates? It is on this score that my interpretations of the Moon phases have diverged most sharply from those given in *Phases of the Moon*. Wergin and Busteed relied much too heavily on the decanate rulers, and thus ended up shoving their examples into preconceived categories. In my own search for the rulers of the phases, I have relied entirely on research. Quite often my research confirmed the traditional decanate rulers. But there were also many cases where the system broke down. For instance, Phase 28, the third Aquarius phase, is supposed to have a Venus rulership. Do Karl Marx, Marlon Brando, Herblock, and C. Wright Mills seem Venusian? I think Pluto is more like it.

Since the decanate rulers have proven unreliable, I haven't tried to tailor my phase descriptions to the traditional decanate system. The planetary "rulers" that I have given each phase are meant to describe the kinds of energy one finds in that phase; they are not meant to establish some new system of rulership. In fact, I have often listed two or more planetary influences for one phase.

Moon Phase Symbols

In the process of studying the Moon phases, I began to see them as distinct pictures. I have some clairvoyant ability—partly innate and partly cultivated. There is nothing particularly amazing about this faculty. It is simply the ability to translate a particular energy into a picture which describes that energy. In many cases, especially with the later phases, these pictures appeared spontaneously, without any effort on my part. With other phases, it involved a process of slow crystallization, with one element after another being added to the picture. At this point, I am more or less satisfied with all of the phase symbols. I have lived with them long enough to feel that they are solid.

As I remember, the first phase that I "flashed" on was Phase 16. This phase includes such figures as Krishnamurti, Yogananda, Rudolf Steiner, Keats, Shelley, Jack London, and Cecil B. DeMille. The picture that suggested itself was a monolithic statue being drawn over rolling logs by hundreds of straining workers. Long after I had come up with this image I discovered that Thor Heyerdahl was a Phase 16. Heyerdahl built a replica of an ancient Egyptian boat which he had pulled to the sea in just such a manner!

While my symbols were arrived at through intuition rather than research, they have also been checked back against the characteristics of the phases. For by analyzing the symbols much as one would analyze a dream, one can arrive at most of the same conclusions about the phases that I did. In fact, when there were peculiarities in the examples, a new look at the phase symbol would often reveal things that I had originally missed.

Notes

1. W. B. Yeats, *A Vision* (New York: Macmillan Co., 1969).
2. Alan Wade, ed., *The Letters of W. B. Yeats* (New York: Macmillan Co., 1955), p. 211.
3. Frances Yates, *The Occult Philosophy of the Elizabethan Age* (Henley on Thames: Ark, 1979), pp. 95-81.
4. Ibid.
5. W. B. Yeats, *Essays and Introductions* (New York: Macmillan Co., 1961), p. 50.
6. George Mills Harper, *Yeats's Golden Dawn* (New York: Barnes and Noble, 1974), pp. 3-24.

7. Alan Wade, ed., *The Letters of W. B. Yeats* (London: Rupert Hart-Davis, 1954), p. 340.

8. Ibid., p. 342.

9. Harper, p. 23.

10. Ibid., pp. 23-25.

11. Ibid., pp. 27-68.

12. Wade, p. 712.

13. Marilyn Busteed, Richard Tiffany, and Dorothy Wergin, *Phases of the Moon* (Boulder, CO: Shambhala, 1976).

14. Paul Foster Case, *The Wisdom of the Tarot* (Richmond, VA: Macoy Publishing Co., 1947).

Chapter Two

Sun, Moon, and Moon Phase

Before one can understand the Moon phases, one must first have an understanding of the Sun and the Moon. Luckily, the human body provides an excellent model for this discussion. In recent years scientists have discovered that the two hemispheres of the brain operate semi-independently of each other. The earliest of these studies identified the left hemisphere as the site of linguistic and mathematical thinking. In fact, for a long time the left hemisphere was simply known as the dominant hemisphere. However, more recent studies have shown that the right hemisphere has its own character and its own strengths—including an ability to visualize spatial relationships, and a sensitivity to moods and emotions. What the scientists were stumbling onto was the age-old difference between solar and lunar perception. The basic breakdown is this:

The left, or solar hemisphere, is associated with linguistic and mathematical skills, logic, abstract thought, and an objective, linear sense of time.

The right, or lunar hemisphere, is associated with sense perceptions, emotional and intuitive responses, spatial, or "global" perception, synthetic thought, and a subjective, or "illogical" sense of time.

The Sun

As the center of our solar system, and the source of all life on our planet, it is impossible to overemphasize the importance of the Sun—either in metaphysics or in astrology. It is the Sun that defines night and day, and the passing of the seasons. Through these most obvious of natural cycles, the Sun awakens us to the fact that there is an order in the Universe—an order that is accessible to the mind.

The Sun is not only the source of all life on the planet, it is also the source of all consciousness. It takes energy to see, hear, touch, smell, taste, and think, and this energy is ultimately derived from the Sun. When the Sun in a person's chart is strong, there is a lot of energy, but there is also a lot of consciousness. Like the Sun, solar individuals try to illuminate everything; they try to make everything clear and rational, regardless of whether this knowledge is of any immediate use. Like the Sun, they would like to command an ever-higher overview of the Creation. They are looking at life in broad daylight, and this necessarily brings the more obvious, external side of reality to the fore. But the very clarity and concreteness of these perceptions also gives them the confidence to act decisively in promoting their own vision of life.

Since it is the Sun's nature to illuminate and reveal, a strong Sun will give an honest and straightforward personality. Solar people are always revealing themselves, and in the act of revealing themselves, they are also finding themselves. Solar individuals are artists, creators, actors, personalities. They are always explaining and expressing themselves. They seem to say: "All of these things, I am—all of these things and more." Solar people are creators, but they are also separate from their creations, for in the act of creating they separate and objectify subconscious impulses, and thus remove themselves from their influence. Solar individuals want total independence. They want to be self-defined, self-motivated, and psychologically self-sufficient. They want to be like the Sun—participating in the material world, but enthroned within the spiritual world—self-created and absolute.

In the astrological chart, the Sun represents the self-conscious center of the personality, around which all other aspects of consciousness naturally revolve. The light of the personal Sun is a direct incarnation of the Light of Lights. It is our most direct link to the Divinity, and as such, naturally assumes the central role in our internal world. The confidence, strength, vitality, and moral force that we need to rule our inner kingdoms are all ultimately derived from our sense of divine origin. The right to be ourselves and express ourselves is essentially a divine right, for in expressing ourselves, we are expressing an aspect of the Divinity. The Sun is the source of all righteousness and virtue, courage and strength. It is the source of righteousness because all true morality is based on the promotion of the life force. It is the source of courage because courage is rooted in an identification with Divinity, and the accompanying sense of spiritual indestructibility that comes with that identification.

On an inner level, the Sun is responsible for putting all of our various psychological drives in order. On an outer level, it is just as much the King—defining the environment, dominating it, and organizing it according to its own hierarchy of values. These values will differ from sign to sign. Virgos are not going to see the same things in the environment as Leos; they are not going to value the same things, or promote the same things. It's not that the Sun itself has changed; it has just been filtered through different mediums.

When the natal chart is fixed at birth, the transpersonal, or divine Sun is shining through one of the zodiacal signs, and it is through this sign that we continue to experience the divine light of the inner Sun. This light will be embodied in our personalities, as colored by a particular house placement, etc. Thus, the Sun sign indicates our basic spiritual individuality, displayed outwardly in our most obvious personality traits, and experienced inwardly in the characteristic way that we think about ourselves.

The Sun is always related to spiritual aspiration, because the individual Sun is always trying to merge with the transpersonal Sun; the "Son" is trying to merge with the "Father." This can occur only as we become successfully centered within our own archetypes. Thus, by learning to express deeper and deeper aspects of our zodiacal archetypes, we move further behind them, to the source of creative energy that generated them in the first place. Solar living is a type of meditation, a type of centering ritual. By finding adequate forms in which to express our archetypal energies, we create a channel through which more of those energies can flow. Thus, people who are true to themselves, who are true to their divine solar natures, are generally also healthy and energetic. Their upright relation to the divine energy within themselves brings them more energy—more energy with which to enjoy life, more energy with which to accomplish their goals and ambitions.

When solar individuals are not living up to their ideal Selves, they often try to fool themselves and the world through boastful, pompous, or arrogant behavior. This is generally as transparent as it is unpleasant. However, even this poor expression of solar energy is preferable to a poverty of solar energy, and the anemic desires, lackluster personality, and self-disparagement that go along with it. At least the braggart has energy.

The Sun represents the power of self-consciousness, the power to know oneself and the purpose for one's existence, and the clarity and force of will with which to achieve that purpose. On a basic level the solar impulse is the impulse to shine in a crowd. It is the desire to attain a central position, a position of high visibility and political or moral dominance. It is also the desire to live life fully—to immolate oneself in the passionate pursuit of one's conscious goals.

The Moon

The solar perspective is essentially religious. Assuming a knowledge of good and evil, beauty and ugliness, it tries to impose its own vision of reality onto the world. Like the solar Hero, it sets itself up against the dark forces of the world in order to establish its own shining vision of the Kingdom.

The Moon, by contrast, is passive and reflective. It assumes a reality outside itself and tries to accurately mirror that reality within its consciousness. The Moon functions best when it is reflecting reality in an accurate and unbiased way, yet it is also fairly comfortable with confusion, ambiguity, and complexity. Lacking the arrogance of the Sun, it doesn't feel a need to understand or control every aspect of the environment. In fact it feels this kind of control is a fantasy. For as we ourselves are a part of nature, our success will ultimately depend on adapting to nature, on moving with its rhythms and going with its flow. The Moon is fertile because it works with potentials that are already present in the environment. It is grounded in nature, and it is helped along by nature—in the biological realm of growth and reproduction, and in the social and spiritual realms as well.

The lunar perspective is tentative and changeable. It is constantly adjusting to shifts in external circumstances, and re-evaluating its perspective in light of new facts or understanding. It is this openness to life that puts the Moon on the cutting edge of the growth process, for like a child, the Moon is always learning; it is always outgrowing old perspectives and evolving new ones.

The explanations for the Moon found in most astrology books are scattered but consistent. They connect the Moon to motherhood and child-rearing, to women in general and mothers in particular. They give the Moon a changeable, moody, and emotional nature, and relate it physically to the stomach and the digestive system. All of these traits are derived from the sign Cancer, the sign traditionally ruled by the Moon. This analogical approach is certainly valid, but it would be a lot more instructive if it were taken a bit further.

The sign Cancer is concerned with the in-gathering of worldly experience. Much as the crab draws in nourishment by pulling food into its mouth, the soul takes in nourishment by internalizing and subjectivizing its worldly experience. Individuals of this sign often value the memories of their experiences more than the experiences themselves. For it is from these memories that they are able to think about life. Memories constitute the real essence of experience; they represent what we have gotten out of an experience—its content or meaning.

The Moon is related to the digestive system. It is responsible for the extraction of nutrients from our food. On another level, however, it is also what extracts meaning or information from our experiences. This information cannot be incorporated in its raw form. Like the food we eat, it must be digested, through rumination and reflection, so that it fits in with or adds to our previous understanding, so that it completes, perfects, or clarifies our inner picture of the world.

Images and Symbols in Lunar Perception

According to Aristotle, sense perceptions must be turned into images by the imaginative faculty before they can really be thought about, for "the soul never thinks without a mental picture."[1] Thus, it is the images of our experiences rather than the experiences themselves that form the raw material of our thoughts.

Centuries later Thomas Aquinas echoed these thoughts, adding that understanding is impossible without imagistic abstraction: "Man cannot understand without images (phantasmata); the image is a similitude of a corporeal thing, but understanding is of universals which are abstracted from particulars."[2]   In other words, we have to simplify or abstract our experience in order to really think about it. This process is quite obvious when we are relating an experience to another person. What is it that we choose to include, and what is it that we choose to omit? What is it that we've missed in the first place? The fact is that we routinely make our lives into a story with characters, symbols, and plot lines. The elements of experience that really draw our attention are those which have some resonance with the archetypes of the unconscious. For when an element has symbolic undertones, it always seems deeper, and more relevant. Without even being aware of it, we turn our experience into symbols, and then organize these symbols into metaphors, stories, and myths. This allows us to really grasp our experience, and to imbue our lives with meaning and continuity.

The Moon's translation of outer reality into inner reality has an interesting analogy in the reception of visual images by the eye. When we see something, it is not the sense object itself that we are seeing, but an image formed by light reflected from the sense object. Actually, the whole reality of a perceived object is a matter of subjective interpretation. We learn to see depth; we learn to see perspective. We even learn how to see right side up, since the image that forms on the retina is actually upside down. Thus, our ability to receive accurate information through vision is a process which is learned through experience.

The picture below demonstrates the translation of an external reality into an internal reality, through the passage of the visual image through the lens of the eye. Notice that the picture includes the double cones which form the central symbol of Yeats' system.

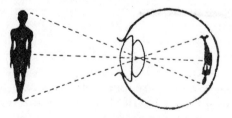

Figure 2.1

Please don't infer from this discussion that the Moon is associated exclusively with the eyes. The Moon processes data from all the senses; in fact it is more closely related to hearing and smell than it is to sight. Its relationship to the senses is also very different from that of the Sun. The Sun views the senses as tools of its will. It also assumes that the information it receives through the senses is accurate, especially information received through the eyes.

The Moon is more suspicious of the senses. It understands how easily internal factors may affect our perceptions of the world—our emotional state, for instance, or our education, age, nationality, or belief structure. And there's also the possibility of conscious deception. Appearances, especially in the social realm, are very different from reality. While the Moon may use sensory information as a kind of framework for its understanding, its final synthesis is based on analysis and intuition. This is to be expected. As a watery "planet" the Moon would naturally use emotion—or emotional intuition—to organize the facts and impressions it has gathered from the environment. This is what makes the Moon so mysterious; it will often pick up on and react to factors in a situation that are obscure or even invisible to others.

In earliest life, we absorb the worldview of our parents and our society. This internal image of the world serves as the model by which we interpret our experience. Without such a model, without some kind of grid-system to separate important from unimportant information, we would be absolutely swamped. We would suffer from sensory overload, and would be unable to function competently in the world.

As we grow older, we add information to this inherited worldview; we revise and perfect it in light of our experiences. Yet the Moon is very conservative, and will often stick with the same basic assumptions for a lifetime. However, if the same unassimilable facts keep coming up, the Moon will sometimes restructure its worldview in order to accommodate them. This process is usually accompanied by a period of deep isolation, for during these periods we are like crabs shedding outgrown shells. The old way of seeing things has been discarded, and the new perceptual grids are not yet in place. We are too open to outside influences, many of which may be harmful to our well-being.

This brings us back to the role of the Moon in mothering. Children grow very fast; their worldviews are constantly being modified or transformed to include new understandings and new modes of behavior. If children are to grow freely they can't be on the defensive all the time. They must have a safe and supportive environment, where they will have enough confidence to cast off their outgrown shells. It is the job of the mother or the mothering parent to create and sustain such an environment.

The passive in the pattern in the D.

The Moon sign in a person's chart always refers in some way to the person's mother, and the way the mother was perceived and reacted to. Positively, it indicates the real strengths—the social and spiritual understandings—which were passed on through the matriarchal lineage. It also indicates the emotional stance a child has inherited towards the world. This will differ from child to child. One child may be receptive to this quality and another to that. This can be seen in the child's Moon sign and in the contrast between the Moon sign and the mother's chart. A child with Moon in Cancer, whose mother has almost no water in her chart, will feel rather emotionally starved and will tend to be very demanding in later life. A child with Moon in Aquarius, whose mother was an eccentric Bohemian, will grow up feeling perfectly comfortable being somewhat odd, living in strange circumstances, or associating with unusual people.

Of course, where a person starts out in life depends a lot on the level of understanding that has already been developed by the parents, and how well this knowledge was transmitted. Bringing up children is serious business, since it is very hard to undo patterns of thought and behavior that were established in early childhood. These patterns are practically somatic; they operate on an unconscious physical level. Thus, if a child's parents neglected its early education, gave conflicting messages, or inculcated bad social habits, the child will have a lot of problems adjusting to the world. And society will also suffer.

The Moon is responsible for maintaining civilization on its most basic level, for it is through the Moon that cultural forms are transmitted from one generation to the next. Like a cup or vessel, the Moon protects the content of civilization from being dispersed in formless, chaotic, or barbaric behavior. It separates, through the threat of ostracism, those who are inside and those who are outside the family and the community—those who are seen as "good influences" and those who are seen as "bad influences." In this the Moon is very conservative. For despite its complexity and cultural sophistication, the Moon is rooted in the survival instincts of the race.

As I have already said, the Moon is responsible for processing perceptual data. The five senses are constantly bombarding the mind with all kinds of data. The Moon has to make sense of all this. If it were to analyze each separate sensation the way the Sun does, it would always be dealing with tiny fragments of reality, and its view would be lopsided and unrealistic. It is the Moon that intuitively connects us with the overall reality of our situation. Thus a poorly functioning Moon is often associated with a poor reality sense or even mental illness (lunacy). Notice that extreme solar types, like scientists and mathematicians, are notorious for their poor understanding of their immediate surroundings.

The Moon sign tells us a lot about the characteristic way in which a person processes perceptual data. Thus, a person who was born when the Moon was in Aries tends to have a lot of faith in first impressions, and is quick to act and react. The Moon in Taurus individual digests conscious and subconscious impressions much more slowly and thoroughly. People with the Moon in Capricorn are slower still, which may explain why they are so cautious in fast-moving social situations: they're not that sure about what's going on around them.

While the Moon sign tells us a lot about perceptual integration, it also indicates the qualities that we value in ourselves, in other people, and in the environment. It shows the kind of experiences we treasure from the past and the kind of experiences that we are aiming for in the future. It shows the kind of values we use to orient ourselves in our passage through life. Without the fixity of the natal Moon, we would be adrift, and life would seem like an endless stream of meaningless events, for it is the natal Moon that narrows down the field of experience to a manageable level. Like a sieve, the natal Moon retains only those experiences that are considered personally valuable. The rest, while of possible value to others, is simply allowed to pass by.

When the Moon is highly developed it does not just react passively to changes in the environment. It also initiates change, weaving a network of subtle influences and connections that help guide events along preferred lines of evolution. People with the Moon in Libra, Scorpio, Aquarius, Cancer, and Sagittarius are particularly adept at this. When the Moon is in more masculine signs, such as Aries, Capricorn, and Leo, it functions with less finesse, attempting to achieve its purposes in a direct and sometimes forceful manner. This is often effective in the short run, but in the long run it can be self-defeating, for it tends to set up obstacles in the environment.

The Moon serves as the gateway between the past and the future. It shows how we conceptualize the past, the present, and the future, and how we navigate within this flow of events. Since the Moon is related to memory, it forms the very basis for our sense of continuity. Through lunar reflection, we can go over the past, and get a sense of how things have generally worked out. By extending these trends into the future, we can get at least a vague idea of where things are headed. Thus, we are in a much better position to chart a course that will meet with little resistance.

While the Moon is not lacking in higher spiritual goals, its visions of the future are more closely related to the fulfillment of basic needs and desires. In fact it could be argued that one of the main functions of the natal Moon is to re-enact or re-actualize the idealized memories of one's most treasured experiences. This is not simply nostalgia. People treasure what they really need, and what they really need is spelled out, to some degree, in their Moon signs.

When the Moon is in Cancer, for instance, there is need for deep emotional relationships, and experiences with a lot of complexity and psychological depth. People with the Moon in Pisces search for experiences that have a transcendant edge to them. People with Moon in Aries look for situations where they can fight for their ideals.

Lunar consciousness is reflective. It allows people to accurately mirror the reality of their situations, and to navigate through those situations safely and effectively. But lunar consciousness also carries its responsibilities, for along with an understanding of a situation comes an understanding of that situation's potentials and needs. The Moon is the ruler of the sign Cancer, and like Cancer, it is naturally helpful and nurturing. Almost without thinking lunar individuals try to create an environment that is conducive to emotional and spiritual growth. The Moon sign, then, also serves as a resource for other people, for though we really need the things designated by our Moon signs, we can generally collect enough of those experiences and enough of that energy to share with others. And that's where the famiily comes in, for in the healthy family there is an open sharing of energies, experiences, and emotions. Through unconscious give-and-take, the family, therefore, can facilitate the development of a more well-rounded, and ultimately more functional attitude towards life.

The Moon Phase
and the Mercurial Principle

Solar consciousness is related to the left hemisphere of the brain, lunar consciousness to the right hemisphere. Since the Moon phase represents the relationship between the Sun and the Moon, one may well ask whether it, too, has a physical correlate, located somewhere in between the brain's two hemispheres. While one's first impulse might be to look for this body in the connective tissues themselves, the pineal gland offers another interesting possibility.

The pineal gland is located between the two hemispheres of the brain, down by the brain stem. Its function is still obscure. It is light-sensitive, and seems to have something to do with a subconscious response to cycles of light and darkness. In certain early amphibians, it was a light-sensitive spot on top of the head, a literal 'third eye.' For this and other reasons, occultists have often compared the pineal gland to the third eye.

The third eye represents the inner, or occult, side of the Mercurial principle, for it gives the ability to see spiritual energies: auras, thought forms, archetypes, and energy flows. The modern astrological tradition has lost sight of this function. It recognizes Mercury as the translator, or scribe of the gods, from its ability to take ideas and perceptions and convert them into words, numbers, and symbols. However, we have forgotten that Mercury, in its evolved form, is equally capable of perceiving and symbolizing the energies and processes of the internal realm.

Because of Mercury's dual nature—its ability to bridge internal and external consciousness—it is the natural link between the solar and lunar consciousness. Mercury is hermaphroditic; it is half-male and half-female. Thus in one of alchemy's most common symbols, we see Mercury as a person with two heads: one a king, representing the Sun, and one a queen, representing the Moon. These two heads can be seen as the two sides of the brain, while the figure of the hermaphrodite is the mercurial consciousness uniting them.

Before confusing you further, I'd like to make it clear that when I talk about the Mercurial Principle, I am not really talking about the planet in the astrological chart, which is symbolically fixed in the position it occupied at birth. The connection between

Figure 2.2 The Mercurial Hermaphrodite standing over the dragon. Simplified from Jamsthaler, Viatorium Spagyricum (1625).

the Sun and the Moon is affected by the Mercurial Principle, the Hermetic Mercury of alchemy, only one aspect of which is represented in the Mercury of the birth chart. The Mercury of the birth chart may be useful in identifying karmic problems in communication and perception, but since the Mercurial Principle is by its very nature fluid and ever-moving, it could not possibly find its strongest expression within the confines of the birth chart. It may work through the birth chart, but as we shall see, its natural home is outside of time and space.

Like metallic quicksilver, the Mercurial Principle has no fixed form or boundary. This fluidity makes it perfectly suited to effect connections between different spheres of consciousness. If the solar and lunar modes of consciousness were unconnected we would have different forms of awareness, but no real intelligence. There would be no dialectic, no comparisons, no dialogue, no interplay of ideas. The Sun and Moon play off each other like light and shadow. If they were unconnected, the world would seem unreal.

• Solar perception—external perception—is totally flat and two-dimensional unless it is connected with a sense of inner meaning, unless it is connected with lunar perception. We find meaning in life when we see things in the outer world that relate to our inner world. In fact, this type of interconnection is found in all our most important life experiences. In the natal chart it is the Mercurial Principle (and not Mercury) that connects the Sun and the Moon, largely through the angle that it throws between them. This angle determines the vibrational frequency that the third eye sees on, and thus colors and defines our soul's perceptions of the world. We are not exactly blind to other aspects of life; they are just in the background. Their outlines are hazy. By contrast, experiences that relate directly to our own phase are highly defined and clearly visible. They are in focus. It is as if the soul, in incarnating, entered into the image of the Moon phase, and that all the figures in the picture were then embodied by real people and real situations, and most particularly by oneself. •

Projection

In early infancy, the soul is still in the process of inhabiting the body. Consciousness is more or less undifferentiated, for it has not yet adapted to the limitations of physical structure. At this time, the Mercurial Principle is still in its natural, fluid state. However, when the infant's eyes begin to focus, the Mercurial Principle also focuses. The angle between the Sun and the Moon fully crystallizes, and the image of the Moon phase clarifies and focuses, opening as a perceptual gateway into the world. As the child grows, it moves further into its body and further into its vision of the world. Now obviously we don't walk around with a symbol dangling in front of our eyes. However, we are projecting images, and we are projecting energy. It is just that we have already moved so far away from the source of these projections that the images have blurred and disappeared through overexpansion. We are actually living in them. We are inhabiting them.

The constellations provide a wonderful screen for the projection of our subconscious fantasies. In the same way, the world provides a screen for the projection of our inner myths. Since we are not really aware of this, it is usually a genuine revelation when we meet the embodied symbols of our myths in the real world. We act as if these things had an independent existence, when actually at least half of what we see originates within our own mind. For even if we have realized that we have a reality construct, it is hard to remember that we actually inhabit it. In fact, if we were capable of that kind of detachment, we probably wouldn't even be here.

The philosophy that I am outlining is essentially Platonic, but unlike Plato, I am not suggesting that you renounce the world and dedicate your life to a contemplation of the archetypes. Since the Mercurial principle is intimately connected with the divine Logos, it is possible, in principle, to access all knowledge through meditation. However, in practice only a few people born at the end of the cycle are sufficiently detached to use such a direct approach. Most people must access their inner knowledge in a dialogue between their inner and outer lives. They may have an experience, then later reflect on it, and draw out its essential meaning. Or, they'll have some idea or image in their mind, and then they'll act on it, or perhaps incorporate it into a work of art. Each phase has a different balance between the solar and lunar modes of consciousness, ranging from the mystical absorbtion characterizing the phases around the new Moon, to the sensory immersion characterizing the phases around the full Moon.

It would be all too easy to bury the phases beneath the moralistic philosophies of the past, from Platonism, to Buddhism, to Christianity. The full Moon phases could be twisted into an underworld of temptation and sensory immersion. The new Moon phases might make a nice heaven. It is tempting, but it would also be a gross distortion of the cyclical approach to knowledge. The phases form a circle, and each part of that circle is necessary to the whole. It is true that the sensory immersion of the full Moon might seem spiritually dead to a person born at the new Moon. But it is also true that the detached quietude of the new Moon may seem pretty lifeless to a person born at the full Moon. Both points of view are valid as far as they go. But they are, after all, just points of view. The problem with most religions and philosophies is that they pretend to occupy a central, universal perspective, when in fact that is almost never the case. By contrast, the "lunar" perspective—as exemplified by astrology—is more tolerant of individual differences. From the lunar perspective, it is enough to develop our own phase characteristics to a high level. It is enough, and it is possible, for we are working with nature, rather than against it.

The Natural Cycle

The Moon phase tells us a great deal about a person's personality, psychology, and perspective. It tells us almost as much as the Sun sign. But the Moon phase also places people within a context greater than themselves, for it indicates the function that they will serve within the larger cycle of nature. The Moon phases form a single, ongoing, natural process. Forms are created in the first phases; they grow in the first quarter, and they come to fruition at the full Moon. In the third quarter, physical forms decay while spiritual forms establish themselves as the new organizing principle. In the fourth quarter, the seed of the new cycle is formed while the husk of the old cycle is cast away. When all of the phases are working in harmony, the wheel of life is strong and beautiful. Heaven and Earth are brought into harmony, as earthly life takes on the shapes of heaven, and the spirit is nourished and strengthened by worldly wisdom. Each individual helps along the flow of the whole through his or her own personal growth, taking consciousness from preceding phases, developing it, and passing it on to later phases. The end product of this process is the evolution of God-consciousness, not just individually, but collectively.

The natal Moon phase both defines and limits our perspective on life, for even with a few progressions of phase, we are still just seeing a fragment of the whole. Because we have only one frame of reference, we tend to experience our own reality as the reality. While this could lead to an intolerant and egocentric attitude, there are also some hidden benefits here, for if consciousness is simply accepted as a fact, there can be little ego-interference. Our Moon phase is therefore expressed quite naturally, as if it were the only way to be. This allows the forces of nature to work through us, and to subtly direct our energies towards the ends of the whole.

Musings of the Dragon

The Moon phase grounds our consciousness in the unconscious; it grounds us in the Earth Soul, and through the Earth Soul to the primitive order at the roots of the cosmos. While these connections are indispensable both to our sense of orientation, and to our ability to survive in the world, the dark moorings of the soul also have their dangers.

As we grow older, the soul tends to become overly identified with the Earth, or, more accurately, with its perception of the Earth. By projecting all of its inner contents onto the outer world, it gradually becomes mired in an overly materialistic view of reality. It dissipates itself in projections, and then finds itself too weak to guide the organism through a tangle of worldly desires. From a paranoid point of view it might seem as if the Earth had become a huge monster eating the soul and chewing it into little pieces. Older cultures have, in fact, portrayed the "unredeemed" aspects of nature in just this manner. Thus, in Figure 2.2, we see the dragon Typhon lying beneath the feet of the victorious Mercurius.

The story of the caduceus sheds some light on this symbolism. In this myth, Hermes, or Mercury, was walking along the road when he came upon two snakes entwined in mortal combat. Striking the ground between them with his staff, the two snakes unwound themselves, and coiled up his staff to form the caduceus. These two serpents represent the Pingala and the Ida—the Sulfuric and Mercurial streams which are the driving forces of the waxing and waning halves of the lunar cycle. Elsewhere these serpents have been represented as a single serpent, or a single dragon, which bites its own tail. The meaning is the same. It is a symbol of nature caught up in the struggle for survival—in fight or flight, desire and fear. The element of desire is strongest in the youthful phases of the lunar cycle. Thus, the waxing phases, in their most unevolved form, are driven by the fiery serpent of desire. Their central motive is the sexual marriage symbolized in the full Moon. By contrast, the waning phases—the phases of old age—are driven by the chilly serpent of fear. Their basic motivation is the preservation of individual consciousness from physical death, as symbolized in the darkness of the new Moon.

On a primitive level, the lunar cycle is no different from the samsaric cycle; it is an endless circle of desire and fear. Such is the consequence of physical incarnation and its accompanying separation of viewpoint. But there are reasons for the soul's incarnation. The soul incarnates to gain experience, to individuate, to grow, to transform its potential consciousness into concrete wisdom. The Mercurial Principle is at one with these higher purposes of the soul. It is therefore able to dominate the dragon of unconscious compulsion, and transform its endless circle of desire and fear into an upward-moving evolutionary spiral.

Figure 2.3 Mercury. Simplified from Valentinus, 'Duodecim Claves' in Musaeum hermeticum (1678).

The Mercurial Principle tames the world of nature and harnesses it to the purposes of the spirit, transforming the lunar cycle from a grinding machine of destruction into a natural pathway of growth and liberation. Looking out on the world from between the eyes, the Mercurial Principle establishes a central spiritual perspective which implicitly defines life in terms of the growth of the soul. The material world loses its hypnotic fascination; it is no longer experienced as an all-engulfing reality, but becomes a field of experience, a field of opportunities and challenges, some portion of which can be used towards the growth of the soul.

The Mercurial Principle gives us enough discrimination to perceive what is and is not appropriate to our personal growth. It also provides a seminal understanding of the specific spiritual processes necessary to the mastery of our own Moon phase. Thus, each part of the cycle is given its own particular magic, and it is this magic that we will be discovering, developing, and sharing throughout our lives.

In Greek mythology, Mercury served as a guide or escort for souls who were entering the underworld. Mercury does, in fact, serve as a guide for the soul, but remember that the underworld of this myth is the world we inhabit, for at least from the perspective of the spirit, the Earth is a dark and twisting cave. Things are not always what they seem, and the soul must exercise constant discrimination to avoid losing its way.

When the Mercurial Principle descends into matter, forsaking its heavenly home to light the way for the incarnating soul, it necessarily sacrifices much of its natural fluidity, for it is essentially crucified in the earthly center of the astrological chart. However, even in this form, it retains its ability to communicate its heavenly message—largely through the angle that it throws between the Sun and the Moon.

The Angles

The angles represent a simple, but powerful, form of mercurial magic. They operate through regular numerological principles, principles which are at the foundation of the entire physical universe. The angles, and mathematical principles in general, communicate divine intelligence to all the forms of nature. This "ensoulment" of nature can either be seen as the fall of the spirit into the captivity of form, or as a sacrificial incarnation of the Logos, calculated to awaken the latent divinity of the Creation. In either case, from the spirit's point of view it represents a loss, for the Divine Logos has traded its pure, archetypal form for the imperfect and transient forms of nature.

As an incarnation of the Divine Logos, the angle between the Sun and Moon contains the seed idea for each of the Moon phases. The meanings for these angles basically follow the same principles that have been delineated in the traditional interpretation of planetary aspects. For instance, Phase 9, which begins when the Moon is 120 degrees ahead of the Sun, has the same easy-going, unconscious quality that is generally associated with all 120 degree angles. Phase 5, which begins when the Moon is 60 degrees ahead of the Sun, is fundamentally a phase of concrete opportunity—quite in keeping with the traditional view of the 60 degree angle.

However, there is a problem. How can we explain the drastic difference between the waxing and waning trines in the Moon phases—a difference which is not mirrored in the traditional interpretation of planetary aspects? To answer this question I did some research, and what I've found is that waxing and waning planetary aspects, as determined by which of the planets is faster-moving, are indeed different, and that these differences are in keeping with the Moon phases. To clarify: A trine between the Moon in Taurus and Jupiter in Virgo is a waning trine because the Moon travels faster than Jupiter, and the angle is therefore closing. It doesn't matter whether the aspect is applying or separating; just that the angle is closing. If, on the other hand, the Moon were in Virgo and Jupiter were in Taurus, it would be a waxing aspect, because the angle between the two planets would be expanding.

Waxing trines, whether between the Sun and the Moon, or between two planets, are characterized by an easy-going, unconscious quality. Waning trines, on the other hand, are characterized by a highly conscious, analytical quality. This quality is found in the Moon phase that begins the waning trine (Phase 19), and in any planetary pair joined by a waning trine. Astrologers simply have been missing the boat in half of their interpretations. This subject is obviously worthy of further investigation.

To recapitulate, the basic intelligence and meaning of each Moon phase is contained within the mathematical angle which defines it. However, one must be very cautious in proceeding on that basis alone. Traditional interpretation of aspects is grossly inadequate, as it fails to make significant distinctions between waxing and waning aspects.

Egyptian Mysteries

The cycle of the Moon phases represents the cosmic mechanism regulating the cycle of creation, growth, decay, death, and rebirth. We are dealing with something of vast significance, so we should not be surprised to find the Moon phases alluded to in the cosmologies of other cultures and other times. One of the most powerful of the lunar visions is found in the Isis-Osiris myth of ancient Egypt.

Osiris was one of the most ancient and revered of the Egyptian gods. He was closely associated with agriculture, and especially the rebirth of vegetation that followed the annual flooding of the Nile. The action of the Osiris myth is initiated when the god Set kills Osiris, mutilates him, and throws his body into the Nile. Grieved at the loss of her husband, Isis undertakes a prolonged search for Osiris, asking after him wherever she goes. Eventually she discovers his body entwined in the roots of a tree. Gathering together its pieces, she embraces the body, and receives Osiris' seed, thus conceiving the Sun god, Horus. When Horus grows up, he avenges his father by killing Set. He then pulls out his own left eye and offers it as a sacrifice to his father, an act which brings about the resurrection of Osiris.

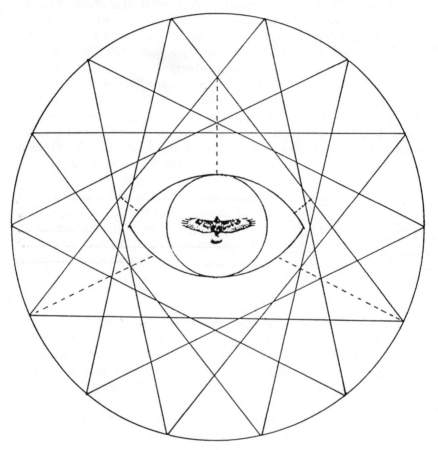

Figure 2.4 Rebirth of Horus in the King's Chamber

There are many variations of this myth. We see it in the Eleusinian mysteries of Greece, with Demeter taking the place of Isis. We see it in the Finnish Kalevala. We see it in the many European fairy tales which center on the figure of a loyal wife who travels the world searching for her husband. The symbolism is all basically lunar. Set represents the Saturnine aspect of the lunar cycle; he is the monster of unredeemed nature, who devours the solar hero and divides him into pieces. The Greeks were later to identify Set with the snake-footed monster Typhon, and it was perhaps from this source that the alchemists derived their dragon.

As for the goddess, Isis, she clearly represents the Moon. Her journey over the face of the Earth, and the gathering of Osiris' body, represents the Moon's journey through the phases, and the gathering together of all the many varieties of worldly experience. The embrace of Osiris' body symbolizes the new Moon—the soli-lunar conjunction—at which time the seed of the old cycle is fertilized and a new solar consciousness is born.

In an alternate version of the myth, Isis is fertilized by Osiris as she hovers over his body in the form of a bird. This version of the myth seems more appealing, probably because it reminds us of the fertilization of Mary by the Holy Ghost. In both of these mythical fragments, the symbol of the bird refers to the Mercurial Logos, as it fertilizes the soul with new spiritual understanding. Fittingly, this fertilization takes place in the Aquarian phases immediately preceding the new Moon. At this stage in the cycle, worldly experience is more or less over, and consciousness is turning back on itself, back to the Mercurial Logos from which all reality is envisioned and created. At this time the limitations of the old perspective are becoming apparent, for the Mercurial Principle is detaching itself from Earth-bound consciousness and regaining its naturally fluid and multi-faceted perspective.

Hovering over the body of earthly experience, the soul can now see how dead it was to life's true meaning. But in this death the soul is also experiencing a resurrection of the Earth's potentials, for its new vision will allow it to re-enter the cycle on a new and higher plane of consciousness.

The Great Wheel *to experience the psychical.*

At this point it may be useful to stop and take a look at the overall cycle. In order to understand the Moon phases, we must first grasp the difference between the waxing and waning phases. Basically the waxing phases are phases of physical incarnation, and natural or biological growth. In the symbol for Phase 1 we see a lotus blossom expanding and opening. Similarly, the keynote for the waxing phases is the expansion and incarnation of spiritual ideas and ideals into the manifest forms of nature, forms which are as numerous as the petals of a lotus.

In the waning phases, physical vigor is on the decline. The soul begins to detach itself from the body and center itself within the spiritual realm. This process is marked by a series of contractions or renunciations, wherein different aspects of earthly experience are mastered and transcended. In the symbol for Phase 15—the full Moon phase—we see a beautiful woman with a diamond necklace falling out of her pocket. The diamonds represent the contraction of worldly experience into clear and valuable spiritual insights. These insights are gradually interconnected and crystallized, as the individual creates an increasingly accurate internal representation of the world. This process of internalization helps the individual to gain control of her psychic projections, and at the same time affords her the understanding she needs to effectively transform the world itself.

People of the waxing phases tend to project reality outside of themselves. They are motivated by an erotic attachment to the beautiful forms of nature—a tendency which finds its ultimate expression in the sexual and emotional relationships of the full Moon.

The waxing phases move towards the reflection of God in concrete form, or, more accurately, the reflection of God in other people. Negatively, these individuals are blinded by desire. They seek form rather than content, and set their sights on goals which are entirely unworthy of their energies. Positively, they are healthy, life-asserting, creative, and loving. They have a natural feel for life, and generally know how to have a good time. They can also go far in creating their own world, for the powerful creative and organizational energies of the Sun are behind them.

While the waxing phases are essentially solar in orientation, the waning phases are lunar. They are much more reflective, adaptive, and emotionally subjective than the waxing phases. They are also a lot more complex.

People of the waning phases are motivated by a desire for spiritual, psychological, and emotional freedom. This tendency finds its ultimate expression in the spiritual rebirth of the new Moon, and the thousand-petaled lotus which is its symbol. Positively, these people are seekers on the path of enlightenment. By constantly re-evaluating their experiences, they are able to achieve a more central and comprehensive understanding of themselves and the world. This understanding, in turn, is used to catalyze the evolution of both psyche and society.

Negatively, waning phase individuals are confused, frightened, and unhealthy. A pervasive fear of death seems to undermine their ability to enjoy life—a fear which is often disguised beneath a cloak of ascetic political or religious philosophies.

Most of the world's religions have a waning phase bias, some more than others. An extreme, but illuminating example can be found in the Gnostic Christian philosophies which proliferated in the first centuries after the crucifixion. According to the Gnostics, the world is evil, and the creator of the world is evil. In fact, if they had known about the Moon phases, they would have said that the entire waxing half of the cycle was demonic, for it is this half that leads the spirit into matter. Never mind the beauty of the world, and the love and happiness that we can find here. The world, the senses, sexuality, and even the soul, were seen as cosmic traps which had been consciously devised to imprison the spirit. The planets, meanwhile, became demonic intelligences under the supreme control of the Demiurge, each one binding the spirit with its own characteristic form of evil. Thus, the descent of the spirit into matter was seen as a fall into Pride (the Sun), deception (Mercury), lust (Venus), indolence (the Moon), aggression (Mars), gluttony (Jupiter), and avarice (Saturn).

In many of the Gnostic philosophies, Christ was explicitly identified with the Mercurial Logos; he was even called "the Messenger." It was His function to awaken that part of the soul which was divine in origin, and safely conduct it through the planetary spheres and on to the Godhead. So far as the waning phases are concerned there is a lot of truth in this, for each of these phases represents a "planetary test" in which some form of renunciation is the only escape. During the waning half of the lunar cycle, the spirit is casting off the psychic skins that it accumulated in the waxing phases, for it is heading towards the divine marriage of the new Moon, which can take place only after the spirit has cast off its final veil. Thus, while the Mercurial Logos has been guiding the soul all along, it is in the Aquarian phases at the very end of the cycle that it is finally stripped of its earthly camouflage and revealed in the fullness of the Inner Light.

• Mercury is exalted in Aquarius precisely because this is the sign in which it is least colored and most detached; in other words, this is the sign in which the astrological Mercury most closely approximates the Mercurial Principle. But even here Mercury must be developed beyond the qualities of the sign—to a state of all-penetrating universality—before we can start talking about the Mercurial Principle.•

In the Aquarian Moon phases, the Mercurial Logos frees itself from the final veils of Earth-bound consciousness. This purification includes an elimination of all zodiacal influences, for even though Aquarius is the most "colorless" of all the zodiacal signs, it is nonetheless a part of the Earth's outermost etheric garment.

In the final phases of the cycle consciousness is regaining its fluidity, as the harsh and discriminating focus of the ego is left by the wayside. Compassion is no longer an ideal to be admired; it is the byproduct of a consciousness which sees nothing but Unity wherever it looks.

Notes

1. Aristotle, *De Anima*, 432 17 (Hett's translations).
2. Thomas Aquinas, *In Aristotelis libros De sensu et sensato, De memoria et reminiscentia commentarium,* ed. R. M. Spiazzi (Turin-Rome: 1949), p. 91.

Chapter Three

How to Find Your Moon Phase

The only information you need to find your Moon phase is the exact position of the Sun and Moon in your birth chart.

First, determine whether you were born during a waxing or a waning Moon. Remember that the Sun and Moon both travel in a counterclockwise direction; they follow the natural order of the zodiac (Pisces, Aries, Taurus, Gemini, etc.). Also remember that the Moon travels much faster than the Sun. So if the Moon is in a later zodiacal sign than the Sun, but has not yet passed the opposition point, you were born in one of the waxing phases (Phases 1 through 14). If the Moon has already passed the opposition point and is now closing in on the Sun, you were born in one of the waning phases (Phases 15 through 28).

All that remains, at this point, is to calculate the exact number of degrees between the Sun and Moon, and to look up the angle in Figure 3.1.

As an example let's take a chart where the Sun is 12 degrees of Capricorn and the Moon is 17 degrees of Virgo. This is a waning phase because the Moon has already passed Cancer—the sign opposite Capricorn—and moved on past Leo and into Virgo. Since there are 30 degrees in a sign, the angle will include:

> the 13 degrees that are left in Virgo
> the 30 degrees of Libra
> the 30 degrees of Scorpio
> the 30 degrees of Sagittarius
> and 12 degrees of Capricorn

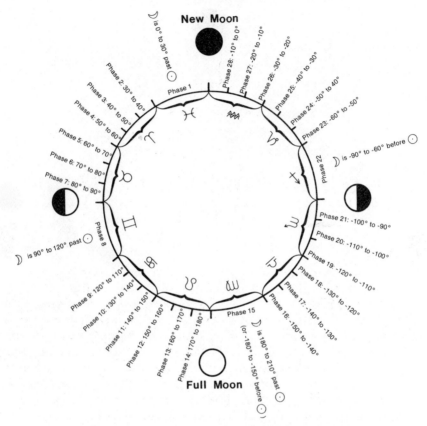

Figure 3.1 The 'Solar' System of Division

Adding them we get 115 degrees, which is actually minus 115 degrees since the Moon is waning. Looking at Figure 3.1, we find this angle within Moon Phase 19, the first Scorpio phase.

These calculations can be done in your head once you have a thorough grasp of the zodiac. For instance, in the previous example Capricorn and Virgo are both earth signs, and therefore trine to each other"—that is, 120 degrees apart. Since the exact 120 angle from Sun 12 Capricorn would be Moon 12 Virgo, the Moon at 17 Virgo just closes that angle 5 degrees, resulting in minus 115 degrees.

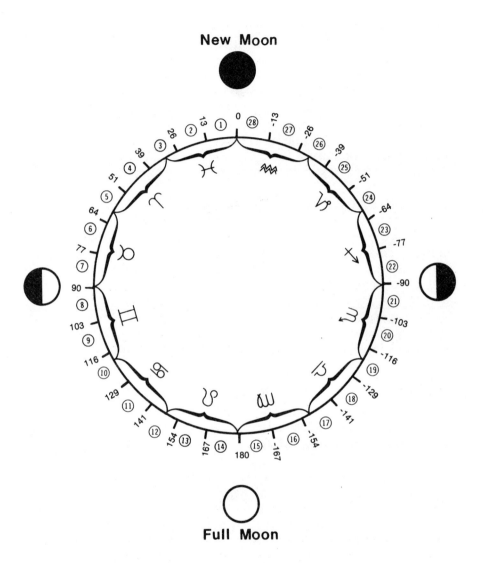

Figure 3.2 The 'Lunar' System of Division

If you were doing a chart where the Sun was 5 degrees Pisces and the Moon was 14 degrees Taurus, you could quickly determine that the Moon was waxing, since Taurus is just two signs ahead of Pisces. To determine the exact angle, you would say that 5 degrees Taurus is the exact sextile (60 degrees), and 14 degrees Taurus is 9 degrees more than that, so the angle is +69. Looking that up in Figure 3.1 you find that 69 degrees is within Phase 5, although just one more degree would put it in Phase 6. In such cases, you should look at both Moon phases, giving weight to the latter.

Progressing through the Moon Phases

My research on the phases made it quite clear that people actually progress from one phase to the next. Since the Moon phases are concerned with psychological and spiritual growth, this is hardly surprising. According to my observations, the central dynamic of a person's life is best represented by the natal phase, or by the next phase if he or she was born on a cusp. However, as a person gets older, there is a tendency to progress, at least on a conscious level, to the next phase. Thus, while people born under Phase 10 may be involved in Phase 10 activities, eventually they will start to anticipate the consciousness of Phase 11. They will put all of their Phase 10 activities within the larger context of Phase 11, and start thinking in terms of completing their Phase 10 karma. The consciousness of Phase 11 will dawn on them from without, and as they grow they will begin to internalize and incorporate it.

From my experience, there is no set way to calculate when or if a person will change phases. Many people remain in one phase all their lives. Others may move on when they have exhausted the potentials of their natal phase"—when new material is needed in order for growth to continue. This is not something that happens overnight. It is a gradual process that extends over many years, and may involve periods of anticipation and backtracking. Changing signs (and elements) seems to be especially difficult. Therefore, I have often found that people who were born in the larger phases (1, 8, 15, 22) remain there for their entire lives.

Some astrologers I have talked to have immediately tried to tie progression through the phases to some mathematical formula. But a real study of the phenomena makes it clear that the process is far too erratic, variable, and individualized to conform to any formula. I have witnessed, in myself and others, quick pushes forward followed by periods of backtracking. It is also very common to see people manifesting the traits of two consecutive phases at the same time. From an internal level, none of this feels arbitrary. The Moon moves on when it is time to move on. It seems to know exactly what it's doing.

A Note on the Examples

In many of the examples I have listed, I had only the birth date and not the birth time. Thus, there are bound to be inaccuracies. Question marks in the examples indicate data that is particularly questionable.

An Overview of the Moon Phases

Phase 1: The Lily Pond (Moon is 0 to 30 degrees ahead of Sun)

Keywords: Child-like innocence and vulnerability; playfulness; serenity and mental clarity vs. craziness; spiritual and psychological understanding; broadening of perspective; reality as Mind.

Phase 2: The Trickster (Moon is 30 to 40 degrees ahead of Sun)

Keywords: Impulse and desire; manipulativeness; desire to affect the world; mischievous humor (devilish, amoral); reality as defined by words and concepts; clever new perspectives; inventiveness.

Phase 3: The New World (Moon is 40 to 50 degrees ahead of Sun)

Keywords: The Edenic world of the young child; spreading goodness and light; developing independence, self-confidence; physical coordination; vitality and radiance; joy of movement; exploration.

Phase 4: The Warrior Priestess (Moon is 50 to 60 degrees ahead of Sun)

Keywords: Socialization and social analysis; fighting to strengthen the ideals of one's country (simplistic ideologies, violence); marshalling social energies; civilization vs. barbarity, reason vs. passion; reality grids.

Phase 5: The Romantic (Moon is 60 to 70 degrees ahead of Sun)

Keywords: Emotional outreach; seeking out significant life experiences; risking pain for love; blossoming of romantic sentiment; developing solid human values; reflection.

Phase 6: The Rebel (Moon is 70 to 80 degrees ahead of Sun)

Keywords: Fighting for personal freedom, both psychological and political; defining one's own frame of values; controlling unacceptable emotions or impulses (crude, hateful); mental discrimination; struggle for social justice.

Phase 7: The Plowman (Moon is 80 to 90 degrees ahead of Sun)

Keywords: Tackling collective problems through cooperative efforts; working through negative situations (immersion); practical accomplishments; potency of action; practical readjustment; realism; integrating mind and body.

Phase 8: The Actress (Moon is 90 to 120 degrees ahead of Sun)

Keywords: Confident projection of personality and point of view; active participation in the drama of life; desire for recognition, and frustrations in achieving it; embodying a new vision of life; developing a successful social persona.

Phase 9: The Gathering of Friends (Moon is 120 to 130 degrees ahead of Sun)

Keywords: Gathering individuals into new social groups; unifying power of human emotion (clannishness, jingoism); attunement to the rhythm and flow of life; trusting the life force; uplifting emotion.

Phase 10: The Architect (Moon is 130 to 140 degrees ahead of Sun)

Keywords: Isolated intellectual growth; piecing together a comprehensive world-view; practical planning; worldly ambition; administrative function of the ego.

Phase 11: The Dream Wedding (Moon is 140 to 150 degrees ahead of Sun)

Keywords: Living out a romantic dream; home and family; ministering to the emotional needs of the public; the healing power of love; unraveling misunderstandings and deceptions; memory.

Phase 12: The Warrior King (Moon is 150 to 160 degrees ahead of Sun)

Keywords: Direct and courageous pursuit of desires; ambition and self-promotion; desire for power (misuse of power); mobilization of personal and collective emotions; idealistic political movements.

Phase 13: The Dancer (Moon is 160 to 170 degrees ahead of Sun)

Keywords: Radiant self-expression; physical vitality; full-bodied enjoyment of life; sexual adventurousness; creativity; talents; establishing a family; centering the personality.

Phase 14: The Vision Quest (Moon is 170 to 180 degrees ahead of Sun)

Keywords: The vision quest; courageous pursuit of spiritual ideals (senseless battles); merging with the higher self; embodying the ideal; drive towards completion; chivalric love; sexual adventures.

Phase 15: The Beloved (Moon is 180 to 210 degrees ahead of Sun, or 180 to 150 degrees behind Sun)

Keywords: Developing quality in personal relationships; honest dialogue; giving an accurate reflection of one's point of view; the individual in society; social reform; inner beauty reflected in outer beauty.

Phase 16: The Procession (Moon is from 150 to 140 degrees behind Sun)

Keywords: Spiritual awakening; religious and cultural movements; invisible spiritual forces that shape the historical drama; exploring the symbolic mind; poetry and mythology.

Phase 17: The Conjuror (Moon is 140 to 130 degrees behind Sun)

Keywords: Sexual power used to intensify romantic relationships, or misused in power trips (corruption, decay);

sublimation; lyrical romanticism vs. sensual excess; developing loyalty to higher ideals, or getting lost in subconscious projections; creations of the imagination; art.

Phase 18: The Angel (Moon is 130 to 120 degrees behind Sun)
Keywords: Transcendence; dispassion; mental poise and clarity; the serene perspective of the higher self; victory of the light force; social idealism; overview of the historical process.

Phase 19: The Wise Serpent (Moon is 120 to 110 degrees behind Sun)
Keywords: The investigative mind; penetration to underlying causes; metaphysical or occult substructure of reality; moral dialectics; use or misuse of political or occult knowledge; the power of words and symbols.

Phase 20: The Forgiven Heart (Moon is 110 to 100 degrees behind Sun)
Keywords: Purifying the emotions through devotion and renunciation; reassessing one's life; re-grasping ones' destiny; humanizing society; compassion; positive vs. negative culture.

Phase 21: The Besieged Cathedral (Moon is 100 to 90 degrees behind Sun)
Keywords: Political and ideological struggles; defending the key elements of one's cultural heritage, or attacking elements that are outmoded; constructing a new world view; sense of social destiny.

Phase 22: The Carnival (Moon is 90 to 60 degrees behind Sun)
Keywords: Experimental, open-minded approach to life; futuristic thought; daring to create one's own myth and live out one's philosophy; waking up to cultural myths; humorous overview.

Phase 23: The Widowed Queen (Moon is 60 to 50 degrees behind Sun)
Keywords: Working on one's karma; freeing oneself from paralyzing personal problems (inertia and depression); self-discipline; productivity; applying the wisdom of the past; confident development of personal resources.

Phase 24: The Magic Realm (Moon is 50 to 40 degrees behind Sun)

Keywords: Reality as a cultural agreement; mischievous intrusion of unforeseen factors; integrating the magical, shadow side of the personality (personality splits); the magical underpinnings of nature.

Phase 25: The Great Teacher (Moon is 40 to 30 degrees behind Sun)

Keywords: Final integration of character; solid understanding of the deeper aspects of existence; taking responsibility for the whole of humanity (partisanship); teaching; drawing from ancient wisdom.

Phase 26: The Pied Piper (Moon is 30 to 20 degrees behind Sun)

Keywords: Breaking away from society; rebels and misfits; getting rid of excess baggage; casting off personal restrictions; going where the action is; following the spirit wherever it leads; Utopian idealism.

Phase 27: The Saint (Moon is 20 to 10 degrees behind Sun)

Keywords: Self-recollection; focusing the inner light; mysticism (wrapped up in sweet dreams); refined sensuality; serenity; forbearance; ministering to people's spiritual needs; harmonization.

Phase 28: The Prophet (Moon is 10 to 0 degrees conjunct behind Sun)

Keywords: Death of the old to make way for the new (destructiveness); visionary attunement to the future; critical junctures in development; inalterable natural and socio-political laws; realistic appraisal.

IMAGE: PHASE 1

Chapter Four

Phase 1: The Lily Pond

"We must take ourselves back to the disposition which we said existed in eternity, to that quiet life, all a single whole, still unbounded, altogether without declination, resting in and oriented towards eternity. Time did not yet exist, not at any rate for the beings of that world..."

Plotinus, *On Eternity and Time*

Pisces Phase: Of the nature of Neptune, Moon, and Mars
Image: A newborn child floating on a lily pad and looking up into the sky. At the side of the pool stands an apple tree, with a yellow snake in its roots.

On a developmental level, Phase 1 is associated with infancy. The child on the lily pad suggests the fetus floating in the womb, surrounded by the Great Dream of existence.

In Phase 1, the individual's field of consciousness slowly expands and clarifies as she awakens to life, wide-eyed and full of wonder. A center is slowly condensing out of a myriad of cosmic influences, delicately unfolding like the petals of a water lily. As yet the self is plastic, tentative. It is reaching idly for an image that will give it truthful expression. There is no urgency to this search; the manifest world seems no more than a playful illusion, a vast playground created by the Overmind for no other purpose than the joy of creation. Essence is everything, and form but an illusion that quickly passes away.

For the Phase 1 individual, Mind is everything, since every manifested phenomena is born within the imagination of the Overmind. The Overmind is infinite in extent; it is as high as the sky and as vast as the sea. By comparison the individual's personal mind seems no more than a small pool—but it is here that she can exercise some control.

The mind is one's permanent home. It can be a domed pleasure palace or a house of horrors, depending on how well one maintains one's natural serenity and balance. The mind of a well-balanced individual is like a calm pool which reflects the environment clearly and truthfully, while the mind of an emotionally troubled individual is more like a whirlpool in which the images of life are grossly distorted by uncontrolled desires and fears.

If the Phase 1 individual starts to lose her mental balance, her instinct is to retreat to the safe haven of nature. There she can relax her defenses and smooth the waves of the mind in quiet contemplation. Often the Phase 1 individual has difficulty in adjusting to urban life, for she has few natural defenses against the disjointed and unsettling sensations that are always pouring in from the environment. She much prefers the simple and uncomplicated life of the country. Actually, her needs are very simple. Being meditatively attuned to the source of life's blessings she seems to magically attract most of what she needs from the environment—including the support and guidance of others, and inexplicably good luck from above.

In Phase 1 the Sun and Moon are more or less conjunct. On a symbolic level this indicates a mind that views the world from one perspective and one perspective only. The Phase 1 individual believes that there is only one reality and that every living thing shares in that reality, whether it is aware of it or not. To other people, the Phase 1 individual may seem very insular, for she is completely immersed in her own particular way of seeing things. In her own mind, however, she is convinced that she is perceiving the one, all-inclusive reality, and that others are simply not as attuned to that reality as she is. This child-like confidence makes her a real cultural initiator, for without doubting herself in the least, she is constantly promoting a fresh new vision of life, and subtly drawing others into her own way of seeing things. Though something of a "problem child," she also acts as a subtle harmonizer, restoring faith between people, countering extremist tendencies, and dissolving crystallized points of view.

There is an innocence about the Phase 1 individual that makes her very vulnerable. Her ego is not quite centered, the boundaries of the personality are not yet fixed, and defense mechanisms may b e primitive and ineffective—ranging from stiff-necked stubbornness, to complete withdrawal. Yet despite this lack of emotional sophistication, the Phase 1 individual is quite evolved on a spiritual level, for she seems to bring the condensed wisdom of the entire previous cycle into her present incarnation. In her understanding of evil, she is as wise as a serpent. Recognizing that the senses deceive, she tries to balance her external perceptions with imagination and intuition, for she realizes that evil will arise whenever the outward manifestations of life come to be valued more than its central essence.

Phase 1 Examples

Carroll O'Connor, actor, Archie Bunker in "All in the Family"
Diane Keaton, actress, starred in *Annie Hall* and *Baby Boom*
Ringo Starr, drummer for the Beatles
Antoine de St. Exupery, wrote *The Little Prince* and *Night Flight*
Pearl Buck, author, wrote *The Good Earth*
Sigmund Freud, founder of modern psychology
Washington Irving, author of *Rip Van Winkle*
Muhammed Ali, heavyweight boxer
Randy Newman, comic songwriter
Art Carney, actor, starred in TV's "The Honeymooners"
Ray Davies, lead singer in The Kinks
Robert Morse, actor in *How to Succeed in Business Without Really Trying*
Cloris Leachman, actress, often cast as a crone
Truman Capote, author, bon vivant, *In Cold Blood* and *Other Voices, Other Rooms*
Agatha Christie, mystery writer, author of *Murder on the Orient Express*
Tom Seaver, baseball pitcher
John Newcombe, tennis star
Ho Chi Minh, Vietnamese revolutionary
Dwight D. Eisenhower, Supreme Allied Commander in World War II, U. S. President

Woodrow Wilson, U. S. President, proponent of the League of Nations

U Thant, Secretary General of the United Nations

Myrna Loy, actress in *The Thin Man* series; worked for United Nations

Lewis Mumford, wrote about civilization and the history of cities

Olivia de Havilland, actress in *Robin Hood* and *The Snake Pit*, a film about a sanitarium

A. H. Maslow, psychologist, psychology of self-actualization

Rollo May, psychoanalyst, wrote *Love and Will*

Jean Piaget, psychologist of child development

Dennis Patrick, deprogrammer for religious cultists

Isaac Bashevis Singer, author of *Gimpel the Fool*

Kahlil Gibran, inspirational poet

Igor Stravinsky, composer, best-known for *The Rite of Spring*

Giorgio de Chirico, surrealist artist

Kurt Weill, composer of *The Three Penny Opera*

Tristan Tzara, absurdist, founder of DaDa movement

Emil Nolde, expressionist artist

Hans Christian Andersen, fairy tale writer

Marianne Moore, poet

Shanta Rao, Indian dancer

Phoebe Snow, singer

Rene Descartes, mathematician who developed analytical geometry

Chapter Five

Phase 2: The Trickster

First Aries Phase: Of the nature of Mercury and Mars
Image: A precocious child plays with a puppet, which he dangles
through the bars of his crib. His left hand is raised above his head,
and holds an arrow, point downwards.

With the onset of Phase 2 the ego suddenly crystallizes out of the
Piscean waters of Phase 1. A chasm opens between the self and the
non-self, the manifest and the unmanifest. The Phase 2 individual
positions himself at the interface of these two worlds, giving him
the ability to manipulate events which are just beginning to take
shape.

Developmentally, Phase 2 corresponds to ages zero through
two. At this stage the child is learning to control his body, and to
manipulate his environment. The senses are sharpening and the
intellect is developing the power of focus and concentration. As the
child becomes aware of his new powers he gains a certain sense of
omnipotence. Like many children of the "terrible twos," he can
become a mischievous little imp, pushing his limits as far as they
will go, and testing his will against the will of his parents.

This is also the stage at which the child is learning to speak,
and with the acquisition of language he begins to piece together the
entire world view of his parents. At first his understanding of this
reality system is sketchy, and he is apt to make a lot of false
assumptions and come to mistaken conclusions. But although he

will occasionally falter and stumble, there are also some real
advantages to this naiveté. Since his perceptions are fresh and
unmediated, he is often able to see ways of solving problems that
had never occurred to anyone else. He is also quick to identify
questionable ideas, and to point out hypocrisy and inconsistencies
of thought; since he is expected to adapt to someone else's mental
system, he thinks it only fair that the system be internally
consistent. This passion for mental accounting follows him
throughout life. Thus as he gets older, he will often take the role of
the social gadfly, reminding others humorously, but pointedly, of
things that they would just as soon overlook.

On the other hand, he himself rarely plays by the rules. He
realizes that reality is somewhat arbitrary, determined largely by
what one chooses to focus on or emphasize. Thus, he tends to
modify his own reality system according to his ultimate aims. He
is quick to see the basic dynamics of a situation, and has no
problem engineering a way to get from point A to point B, but he
is in such an early phase that he can rarely see more than a few
steps in advance, and is often thrown off balance by unforeseen
factors. Then, instead of playing the omnipotent sorcerer as he
would like, he ends up playing cosmic dodge ball, as he tries to
avoid the repercussions of his ill-advised actions.

Negatively, the Phase 2 individual is entirely amoral. Rather
than channeling divine intelligence, he uses his intellectual gifts for
selfish ends. Lying, trickery, and evasion are employed without
hesitation if he feels they will get him what he wants. And if he gets
caught he behaves like a child—readily admitting he was wrong,
but also appealing to a kind of parental forgiveness: "After all, I'm
still just a cute and lovable kid" (even if he is fifty years old!).

While the Phase 2 individual can usually get away with a lot,
his tricky, slippery, mercurial intelligence eventually gives way to
principled thinking, as he realizes that good motives lead to good
ends and bad motives lead to bad ends. In no other phase are
karmic effects so clear. This is not surprising, for the moral
principle and the reality principle both amount to the same thing:
if you don't play by the rules you get burned.

On a mythological level Phase 2 is associated with the fall of
Lucifer, for it marks the separation of an independent will from
the spiritual whole. In Phase 2 the desire to manifest destroys the
spiritual balance characteristic of Phase 1, setting up a series of
chain-reaction events that will not come to an end until Phase 15.
During this half of the cycle the individual will be moving out into

the world, and developing and expressing all of his personal potentials. The divine spirit is becoming incarnate, kicked off by the individual's desire for personal identity and personal power.

Phase 2 Examples

Jimmy Carter, U. S. President. (Many recent U. S. Presidents were born with a waxing Moon around the 30 degree mark, including Jimmy Carter, Richard Nixon, Lyndon Johnson, and Dwight Eisenhower. The Phase 2 impulse for control may be one factor, but I also suspect that the United States, at least at present, is a Phase 2 country.)

Carl Sagan, astronomer, popular science writer

B. F. Skinner, behaviorist psychologist; *Beyond Freedom and Dignity*

Julia Child, TV chef

Seiji Ozawa, orchestral conductor

Glenn Seaborg, nuclear chemist, isolated Plutonium

Art Buchwald, political humorist

Gloria Steinem, feminist leader and author

Elton John, rock singer and songwriter

Lucien Stryk, translator

Shari Lewis, ventriloquist

Arthur C. Clarke, science fiction writer, author of *Childhood's End*

Rudolf Arnheim, psychologist of art, wrote *Art and Visual Perception*

James Frazier, folklorist, author of *The Golden Bough*

Daniel Schorr, controversial journalist

George Schulz, economist

Jean Stapledon, actress on TV and Broadway

Carlo Carra, futurist artist

Joe Rauh, lawyer

Alan King, politically-oriented comedian

Richard Pryor, comedian

Jerry Lewis, comedian

Bob Hope, comedian

Eric Satie, composer, cafe pianist, wit

Foghorn Winslow, child actor with deep voice

Margaret O'Brien, child actress

Erroll Flynn, actor, rake

D. H. Lawrence, author, wrote *Lady Chatterley's Lover*
William Simon, economist
Cesar Romero, actor, played The Joker on "Batman" TV series
Rex Harrison, actor, played Henry Higgins in *My Fair Lady*
King Vidor, film director
Rita Moreno, dancer, comedienne
Bernard Montgomery, W.W.II tank general
Teillhard de Chardin, monk turned geneticist, geologist
Bernadette Devlin, Irish nationalist
Prince Bernhard of the Netherlands, power manipulator
Fishbait Miller, doorkeeper for the House of Representatives

Chapter Six

Phase 3: The New World

Second Aries Phase: Of the nature of the Sun
Image: A girl, and a boy pulling a red wagon, run down a hillside to the sunny valley below. A mocking bird urges them on down the path.

The eyes are now fully focused, and the individual stands on the edge of beautiful new world. Life is opening before her as a glorious adventure, an exciting story in which she is playing the lead role. In Phase 2 she was still poised between the manifest and unmanifest; she now plunges wholeheartedly into life. She gives a resounding "Yes!" to the creation.

Entering into the world with the unquestioning trust of a child, the Phase 3 individual meets everything with a mixture of familiarity and wonder. While other people may find her high expectations and sunny optimism unrealistic, this uncompromisingly positive approach to life actually works very well. By seeing the best side of everyone she meets, and seeing the most positive possibilities of every situation she enters, the Phase 3 individual is able to draw the very best out of life. She can travel into the darkest and most hostile circumstances and emerge unharmed, for she is shielded from evil by the protective aura of her own simple faith. At best the Phase 3 individual serves as an emissary of the central spiritual Sun. In her travels around the world, she spreads the light of peace and brotherhood, and awakens the creation to the joyous song of life.

On a developmental level, Phase 3 is related to the child's first attempts at walking. It is here that she experiences the thrill of physical mobility. It is here that she realizes that the world is hers to explore. In Phase 3 the light force is coming down to Earth; the spirit is entering fully into the body. On the lowest level this process can be seen in the development of physical coordination. The Phase 3 individual is training her body to respond to the commands of her will, for she realizes that until she has achieved a certain level of physical coordination and practical competence, she will be unable to enjoy the worldly freedom and independence she so desires. Objective freedom is not possible without self-confidence. However, true self-confidence can arise only when there is an unwavering ascendancy of the spiritual will. Ultimately it is this sense of dependable self-mastery that the Phase 3 individual is trying to develop.

Phase 3 represents a period of rapid growth. Competence and confidence are being developed on many different levels at the same time. Because the Phase 3 individual is changing too fast to develop a particularly unique personality, it is best for her to rely on pre-existent role models and concentrate her energy on internal growth processes. Most of the time she can just enjoy herself and let nature take its course. She should just try to take advantage of her opportunities for growth, and make sure that her mind and body are developing at about the same rate.

While it may seem as if the Phase 3 individual is engrossed in the world, she is actually inner-directed, for part of her consciousness is always looking back towards the light of the Creator. Thus, even when she looks outwards she is able to see the light of the Creator in the Creation. The world of the Phase 3 person is the simple and beautiful world of childhood; it is like the Garden of Eden, for she has not yet fallen from grace by lustfully eating the golden apple of the senses. Realizing that the sin of the Garden was not disobedience but selfishness of heart, the Phase 3 individual shares all of her pleasures with God and with other people. She is open and generous with her energies, flooding her surroundings with a delightfully clean and invigorating radiant energy, like the sunshine of a fresh spring morning.

In Phase 3 we can see the exalted quality of the Sun in Aries, for the Phase 3 individual is embodying a pure radiant energy which has not yet been tied down to any particular form of expression. The Phase 3 individual is free to radiate anything and everything, to do anything and everything. Inwardly her sphere is the entire zodiac; outwardly it is the whole world. She is pure potential, pure promise, a drawn bow ready to burst into energetic activity.

Phase 3 Examples

Julie Andrews, actress, played in *The Sound of Music* and *Mary Poppins*

J. R. R. Tolkien, author of *Lord of the Rings*

Orville Wright, inventor of the airplane

William Shatner, actor, Captain Kirk in "Star Trek"

Edgar Cayce, psychic, healer

Paul McCartney, composer/musician, member of The Beatles. Linda McCartney, his wife, is also a Phase 3.

Pete Seeger, folk singer

Burt Bacharach, songwriter

Elvis Presley, rock and roll singer, cult idol

Maureen O'Hara, actress

Lillian Russell, actress, "Diamond Lil" of Gay Nineties fame

Fred MacMurray, TV and film actor, starred in "My Three Sons"

June Lockhart, actress, best known for her TV roles in "Lost in Space" and "Lassie"

Jose Feliciano, blind pop singer

Richard Benjamin, actor, "Quark"

Alan Bates, actor

Art Linkletter, TV host of "People Are Funny"

Leonard Matlovich, fought for gay rights in the armed services

Jr. Wells, soul musician

Magic Sam, blues guitarist

Jeff Beck, guitarist in The Yardbirds

Arthur Sullivan, composer of Gilbert and Sullivan fame

Tokyo Rose, taunted U.S. troops over the radio during World War II

Henry S. Williams, organizor of the first Pan-African conference

Frances Chichester, sailed around the world in a sailboat

Anne Armstrong, ambassador to England

Jules Piccard, oceanographer

Gordon Cooper, astronaut

Richard Tregaskis, war journalist, wrote *Guadalcanal Diary*

Roger Vadim, movie director, directed *Barbarella*
Roger Zelazny, science fiction writer, author of *Lord of Light*
Rudolf Diesel, inventor of the diesel engine
Ferdinand Porsche, auto designer, manufacturer
David P. Reynolds, of Reynolds Aluminum
Ray Kroc, founded McDonald's empire
Eric Maria Remarque, author of *All Quiet on the Western Front*
Alexander Calder, sculptor, known for his mobiles
Thurgood Marshall, first Black to sit on the Supreme Court
Roscoe Drummond, journalist who broke Joseph McCarthy's grip
Pierre Renoir, impressionist artist

Phase 4: Hephaistos and Athena are the Greek god and goddess associated with this phase. They were often portrayed together, probably because they were both thought to be the progeny of a single parent: Zeus in the case of Athena and Hera in the case of Hephaistos.
    illustration by B. Sauer, 1899

Chapter Seven

Phase 4: The Warrior Princess

Third Aries Phase: Of the nature of the Moon, Jupiter, and Mars
Image: An Egyptian priestess dances on a precipice. Below, a scribe is recording the ceremony.
Expanded Image: The gateway of a walled city, guarded by two female sentries armed with spears. A priestess dances on the roof of the temple, her sheer dress blowing in the wind. In her upraised hands she holds a bow, mirrored by the crescent Moon directly above. Outside the gate, a dark man, wearing a close-fitting cap, inscribes characters on a golden ceremonial shield.

By Phase 4 the individual can no longer imagine himself master of his fate. He has discovered that all of his actions take place within a social context. To preserve his mobility and his potency of action he must now undertake a thorough analysis of the entire social fabric—its laws and customs, its political and religious beliefs, its storehouse of ideas and symbols.

In the image, the gateway refers to the Moon's function in admitting or excluding people from society. Through the threat of ostracism, the Moon separates those who are inside and those who are outside the family and the community—those who are seen as "good influences" and those who are seen as "bad influences." The Moon is responsible for preserving civilization on its most basic level, for it is the Moon that weaves cultural artifacts into the fabric of accepted custom and usage, and thus prevents society from backsliding into barbarism.

In the image, the priestess's swaying body represents the primitive truth of the natural world. The religious context of her dancing and the ceremonial dress she is wearing are cultural forms that *veil* the sexual content of her dance, binding potentially dangerous natural energies, and directing them towards socially useful ends. It is the mind that performs all of this, for the mind holds within itself astral, or mental images corresponding to all the external artifacts and symbols of one's culture. In the mind, the priestess is a goddess; she is seen as a sexual object only if one has failed to internalize society's symbolic code.

The dark man seeks entrance into the walled city. He brings a unique gift—a golden ceremonial shield inscribed with writing. It is a beautiful gift, but also a subversive one, for writing and metallurgy will bring about the downfall of the lunar priestess and the matriarchal society she represents, replacing it with a *solar* society, and its characteristically hierarchical and militaristic style of organization. The problem, then, is one of assimilation. How many cultural forms or spiritual principles can a society assimilate without compromising its basic institutions?

Many persons born under this phase are impatient for change, and wish to remake society according to some new framework of political or spiritual analysis. The alien quality of their ideas, however, will often prevent them from getting very far. There also may be an element of bad faith involved—of destructiveness and subversion—for people generally want to change society when they aren't comfortable in it, when they don't fit in.

At the other extreme we find people who resist any and all social change, or even look backwards towards some previous form of social organization. Suspicious of anything new or foreign, they are content to act as society's sentinels.

In the image, the male and female figures represent the two poles of consciousness around which the Phase 4 individual weaves his analysis of society. The priestess represents knowledge gained through the subconscious mind. This would include dreams and visions, and also the ability to visualize abstract patterns in nature. The bow in the priestess's hand, for instance, has been patterned on an *internal conception* of the crescent moon.

The metal-worker, meanwhile, represents the masculine side of the thought process. Here we see the rational mind as it tests out its abstract theories in the real world.

The mind of the Phase 4 individual has two poles: masculine and feminine, the feminine side representing conceptualization and symbol-formation, and the masculine side representing the concrete application of knowledge in arts and crafts.   On a collective level, the appearance of dialectical thinking represents a tremendous breakthrough, for *abstract thinking* is behind every invention that has elevated humanity beyond the natural state. By the same token, this type of analysis introduces an inherently violent and dualistic consciousness into the world, for it separates humankind from nature. The priestess, in fact, represents the last link to the instinctive natural attunement of the early phases.

At best, the Phase 4 individual has a refined analysis of society that *rings true* because it is in close conformity to things as they are. His words speak from the situation itself, and others listen and defer to his judgment. Like the priestess, the Phase 4 individual commands the right to speak for society, and to direct its course of action. If he can succeed in gaining admittance to society's inner circle, his words, his actions, and his gifts will undoubtedly have a resounding impact.

Phase 4 Examples

Martin Luther King, Jr., civil rights leader, minister

Murray Bookchin, anarchist theoretician, author of *The Ecology of Freedom*

Robert Graves, poet, wrote *The White Goddess* and *I, Claudius*

Charles Fourier, utopian social theorist

Alcide de Gaspari, Italian premier, saved Italy from communist control after World War II

Neville Chamberlain, statesman, appeasement policy towards Hitler

Clarence Gilbert, juvenile judge

James Fulbright, U.S. Senator, established foreign exchange program for students

Plisetskaya, ballerina

Claude Levi-Strauss, anthropologist

Ralph Ellison, author of *The Invisible Man*

J. Edgar Hoover, long-time head of the FBI

Indira Gandhi, Prime Minister of India

William Arthur Garrity, "busing judge" in Boston

Felix Frankfurter, Supreme Court Justice

Alan Alda, actor, best known for his role as Hawkeye on TV's "M.A.S.H."

William Proxmire, muckraking U. S. Senator

Sun Yat-Sen, revolutionary leader, first president of China
Chiang Kai Shek, military dictator of China
Werner von Braun, rocket engineer
Emmaline Pankhurst, feminist
Shirley Chisholm, congresswoman
Alfred von Krupp, German industrialist, produced steel and armaments
Laura Nyro, singer, songwriter
Andre Breton, symbolist poet, founder of the surrealist movement
Yves Tanguy, abstract artist
Jean-Louis Barrault, mime
Octavio Paz, surrealist author, wrote *The Labyrinths of Solitude*
Eugene Ionesco, absurdist playwright, author of *Rhinoceros*
H. P. Lovecraft, horror story writer
Joan Miro, surrealist artist
Paul Taylor, dancer, choreographer
Oleg Cassini, fashion designer
Wolf Messing, psychic, noted for telepathic domination
Emil Jannings, actor, played in *The Blue Angel*
Ken Russell, surrealist filmmaker, made *Tommy* and *Lisztomania*
William Shockley, physicist, inventor of transistor, advocate of white superiority
Nikki Giovanni, writer, authored *Gemini*
Joseph Goebbels, Nazi propaganda minister
H. P. Blavatsky, occultist
Sam Jaffee, actor in *Gunga Din*, also played Dr. Zorba on TV series "Ben Casey"
Osvald Villard, editor of *The Nation*

Chapter Eight

Phase 5: The Romantic

First Taurus Phase: Of the nature of Venus and the Moon
Image: A flower peddler standing by a stone archway. Smiling through tears, she offers a bouquet of roses to a passerby. A mature, attractive woman, she has curly hair, and an ample figure. At her side is a child of about eight years old.

With the onset of Phase 5 the soul is suddenly flooded with powerful romantic emotions and fantasies. The first loves and first heartbreaks are experienced, with new love springing quickly out of the grave of old relationships. Developmentally, the phase is related to the crisis of puberty. This is a poignant stage , when each moment seems like a death or a rebirth, a lost opportunity or a blossoming of new life. The challenge of the age is to remain vulnerable and open to life in the face of growing experience.

The abstract ideas of Phase 4 now seem rather academic. It is time to test out some of these ideas in real life—to flesh them out with experience and worldly wisdom. Ideas will be of little value now; what one needs is the courage to enter fully into life.

The Phase 5 individual always seems to find herself standing at some gateway in life, with new experiences beckoning to her from all sides. Her problem is to decide which experiences to open herself to and which experiences to shut out. Basically, she must trust her feelings, moving towards those experiences which seem attractive and promising, and away from those experiences which seem ugly and unpleasant. Since she can never be sure, she has to open up occasionally and show some trust in life. It is really a matter of approach. If she brings her best to a situation; if she expects the best, and takes only the best out of it, then practically any experience can be positive. Some experiences may be a little hard to digest, but if they are really substantive she will do well not to pass them by.

Phase 5 is the first phase to exhibit true self-reflectiveness. At the end of each day the Phase 5 individual chews over her experiences and extracts their deeper meaning. Initially much of what she has learned is in the form of subconsious impressions and feelings. These feelings are then isolated, identified, and consciously analyzed. If they are deemed of no real value, they are rejected. Otherwise she digests them as best she can.

This is the first phase to give a real awareness of the passage of time. Thus in the image, we see two generations—the mother as a symbol of experience, and the child as a symbol of innocence. The woman remembers all of the varied experiences of her life, and how they have changed her. But she also protects and cherishes her child-self. For that is the most trusting and loving part of her personality, the part of her personality that has retained its excitement about life and all its possibilities.

The Phase 5 individual sees life as a great gift, and she means to receive this gift fully and gratefully. Never content to stand on the sidelines, she is generally a passionate and creative participant in life. She may, at times, suffer deep emotional pain, but she is a spunky and resilient character, so smiles and sunshine quickly follow upon the storms. At home with common people, at home with life, her common sense and street savvy mature with time into serenity and gentle wisdom.

Phase 5 Examples

Anna Magnani, passionate Italian screen heroine
Woody Allen, comedian and film director, won Academy Award for his film *Annie Hall*
Sergei Rachmaninoff, pianist and composer
Benjamin Spock, baby doctor, political activist
Neil Simon, playwright, author of *The Odd Couple, The Sunshine Boys,* and *The Goodbye Girl*
Maria Montessori, educator

Montgomery Clift, actor
Ava Gardner, actress
Leon Russell, rock singer
Liv Ullman, actress, starred in many Bergman films
Ingmar Bergman, film director
Dwayne Hickman, actor in the "Dobey Gillis" TV series
Joel Grey, actor, played Master of Ceremonies in *Cabaret*
Marcel Marceau, mime
George Burns, comedian, actor
Michael York, actor, played in *Cabaret* and *Logan's Run*
Bernie Taupin, songwriter for Elton John
Dietrich Fischer Dieskau, tenor, lieder specialist
Martin Buber, theologian, author of *I and Thou* and *Pathways in Utopia*
Arlo Tatum, pacifist
Jack Vaughn, Peace Corps chief
Andrew Young, ambassador to the U. N. under Carter
Alice Liddell, the original Alice in Wonderland
Bill Cosby, comedian
Bette Davis, actress, starred in *Jezebel* and *The Three Faces of Eve*
Sandy Koufax, baseball superstar
Leadbelly, blues musician
Fats Waller, jazz pianist, humorist
Ben E. King, blues musician
Gary Gilmore, convicted murderer, executed at his own request
James Cagney, actor, 'tough guy' of gangster films
Adlai Stevenson, statesman, U.S. ambassador to U.N.
Willie Nelson, country music singer
Pierre Bonnard, impressionist artist
Edna Ferber, writer, author of *Showboat*
Lew Ayres, actor, played in *Johnny Belinda*; spiritual seeker, pacifist
John Denver, pop singer
Sissy Spacek, actress, starred in *Carrie* and *Coal Miner's Daughter*
Johnny Mercer, songwriter, wrote "Moon River"

IMAGE: PHASE 6

Chapter Nine

Phase 6: The Rebel

Second Taurus Phase: Of the nature of Saturn, Mars, and Mercury
Image: a Roman prison. A helmeted guard sits by the door, a key ring at his belt and a sword in his hand. In the foreground, two prisoners plot their escape.

At this point in the cycle, the social institutions of the previous generation have become hopelessly out of step with the actual needs and desires of the people. They have become a wooden prison—a shell—completely devoid of the spirit that originally framed them.

For the Phase 6 individual, social injustice is not just an abstraction; it is an inescapable memory of his own victimization and oppression. His rebellion against society's rules and values is, therefore, immediate and personal. If he doesn't do something to regain his freedom, he is not going to have enough room to breathe or to grow.

Although the Phase 6 individual would like to lay the foundation for a just society, as an early phase he is in no position to do so. Much of his energy is directed outwards—in an impulsive attack on social injustice, and the political and social structures that support it. However, he is also attracted to psychology, for he realizes that society exercises its most effective control through the subconscious mind—through the way it *frames* reality, and interprets thought and behavior.

Until now, the individual's experience was routinely evaluated according to values and definitions inherited from his parents and his society. At Phase 6 he begins to analyze these unconscious values, images, and myths and bring them into the light of his conscious mind. This new framework of analysis will become the emotional and psychological foundation for his personality—a foundation that is solid because it is in keeping with his natural character.

The main task here is individuation, however, the Phase 6 individual never loses his strong connection to the collective. By keeping an ear to the ground, he is able to stay in touch with the emotional and intellectual stirrings of the masses. He can even serve as a leader or a mouthpiece, though spiritually speaking this is a dangerous proposition—at least until he has firmly established his psychological independence. There are many voices around us; there are many voices *in* us. But eventually the individual must find his own voice, his own truth, his own criteria. The Phase 6 individual may listen to the voices of others, but he must ultimately obey the voice of his own higher self.

In the image, the helmeted guard represents the rational ego, holding the sword of mental discrimination. It is through mental discrimination that the individual divides the true from the false, the valuable from the useless, and the honorable from the shameful. It is through mental discrimination that he judges what he will use and what he will reject in laying out the internal guideposts of his personality. The guard is like a censor, who monitors the subconscious input of society, and all the underlying values and ideas found within it. If it were not for the unblinking vigilance of this internal censor, the individual's own values and agenda would be slowly undermined, and he would imperceptibly sink into the unconscious conformity of the masses.

Usually the Phase 6 individual is a fairly private person. Though he would like to appear open and accessible, at least on an emotional level, on an intellectual level he is quite stubborn and self-contained. Not only has he rejected many of society's values, but he also holds to opinions and emotions that are socially unacceptable, and may even have to be hidden from view. Since he tends to judge people in terms of the system of values they unconsciously impose on reality, he is never quite comfortable with people who don't agree with him.

Taken to an extreme, the Phase 6 individual processes all his experience according to some fixed and rigid ideology. In this way he becomes less, rather than more connected to reality. His isolation deepens, and he develops irrational and eccentric patterns of thought. If he then allows his emotions to get the better of his intellect, a degeneration of personality may result, for the animal nature is too close to the surface in this phase to allow for a careless relaxation of self-control.

A few more words on the psychoanalytical side of the phase. Not only is this person's imagination very strong, but he also has easy access to the archetypes of the collective unconscious. It is because these archetypes are so psychically riveting, and tend to get mixed up with the personal unconscious, that psychosexual complexes are so difficult to dislodge. Merely shining some light on these complexes is rarely effective. The individual could go over them mentally a million times without being able to change them. If, however, he materializes these unconscious contents in some form of physical or artistic activity, he is likely to have more success. This comes very easily here, for the archetypes themselves are a form of mental matter, and only need to be given a *more* concrete form. Once the individual has something concrete and external to work with, the psyche becomes a little more fluid. He is able to work with the internal by working with the external—a principle known to both play therapy and alchemy.

Phase 6 Examples

> Anne Frank, diarist, victim of Nazis
> Charles Manson, cult leader, criminal
> Charlton Heston, actor, starred in *Planet of the Apes* and B*en Hur*
> Moshe Dayan, Israeli Minister of Defense
> Simone de Beauvoir, writer and existentialist, author of *The Second Sex*
> Johnny Carson, talk show host
> Bruno Bettelheim, psychologist, survived concentration camp, works with autistic children
> Pavel Tchelitchev, artist, "In and Out"
> Josef Albers, abstract artist, did "Homage to the Square" series
> Egon Bretscher, nuclear physicist
> Robert Shelton, ex-head of the Ku Klux Klan
> Bernard Fall, leftist historian
> Kate Millett, feminist, author of *Sexual Politics*

Howard Cosell, sports announcer

Matthew Ridgeway, soldier

James Abourezk, radical congressman, resigned in disgust

Anne Bancroft, actress, starred in *The Miracle Worker* and *The Graduate*

Tony Sarg, puppeteer

Karl Nikolaiev, psychic

John Lennon, composer/musician, member of The Beatles

Alfred Hitchcock, filmmaker, director of *The Birds, Psycho* and *Rear Window*

Tom Watson, populist leader in the South

Alfred Adler, psychologist

Anna Louise Strong, American Maoist in China

Al Capone, gangster

Wallace Budge, Egyptologist, *Book of the Dead*

Pier Paolo Pasolini, filmmaker

Leonor Fini, erotic artist

Wendell Stanley, virologist

Julio Cortazar, writer, author of *Hopscotch*

George Santayana, writer, philosopher

Szent-Gyorgyi, biochemist, studied oxidation processes and vitamin C

Julius Lester, writer, *Look Out Whitey! Black Power's Gon' Get Your Mama*

Phil Lesh, musician, member of the Grateful Dead

Gladys Knight, soul singer

Modest Moussorgsky, composer, *Night on Bald Mountain* and *Pictures at an Exhibition*

John Baird, scientist, early developer of television

Sir Francis Bacon, early propagandist for science, statesman of the Elizabethan era

Doris Day, actress, starred in *Pillow Talk*

Chapter Ten

Phase 7: The Plowman

Third Taurus Phase: Of the nature of Mars and Pluto
Image: The sun-dappled hills of a collective farm. In the
background, a man leads an ox out to plow. In the foreground a
muscular man overlooks the scene. He is bare to the waist, and
leans on a staff entwined by a serpent.

In Phase 6 the individual struggled to free herself from internal
and external restrictions. But once these crises have passed, she is
able to relax and take a broader view of the future. She now
realizes that the job of materializing her long range goals will be a
long and difficult one, and that her progress will depend largely on
her ability to work *with* the situation rather than against it. Like
Hercules standing before the Augean stables, the Phase 7
individual faces huge collective problems that can be solved only
by huge collective efforts. Spurred by her deep concern for
humanity, she tackles these problems head on, making up for her
lack of superhuman strength with stubborn persistence and hard
work. To be really effective she is going to have to get help from
others, so she tries to stay within the good graces of the
community, and plays the role of reformer or "loyal subversive"
rather than revolutionary. One finds many Phase 7 s involved in
some kind of social work—in educating the masses, in alleviating
poverty and sickness, or in countering the effects of human
corruption and hate.

While she is willing to listen to many different philosophies and viewpoints—even those of other cultures—the Phase 7 individual is basically a pragmatist. She begins all of her projects with a thorough and honest assessment of her situation, of her capabilities, and of the people with whom she has to work . This gives her a basis for evaluating her progress and her methods later on. For while she is quite willing to take on the hardest of labors, she is no glutton for punishment. If she can devise a method that will get the job done with less effort, she will certainly channel some of her energy in that direction.

The Phase 7 individual tries to use all of her resources to best advantage. Like a farmer cultivating the earth, she cultivates the best qualitites in her own character, in other people, and in her community or nation. She works to transform the coarse into the fine, the useless into the useful, the base into the noble, and the dark into the light. Just as a farmer harnesses the strength of the bull to pull the plow, the Phase 7 individual is able to use gentle persuasion to channel physical and sexual energy into socially productive work. She often has a pacifying, "domesticating" influence on those around her, for her accessibility and honesty, her decency and solid character, evoke the trust and respect of others.

Negatively, the Phase 7 individual fails to maintain an overview of life. She allows herself to get buried in her work or in other physical activities. Rather than directing collective efforts, she sinks into the crowd, and even begins to affect their ignorance and coarseness.

In the image, the staff entwined by the serpent refers to Phase 7's healing power. Exoterically, it is the caduceus of the medical profession. Esoterically, it is the serpent power, which when directed through the natural channels of the body, can heal physical illness, and transform the "dead" earth of the psychically-blocked body into luxuriant strength and vitality. The physical emphasis of the phase also points to the importance of exercise, dancing, and sex to this process, for these are the most natural ways to break up psychic blockages.

Phase 7 Examples

Kathe Kollwitz, artist whose work depicted themes of war, suffering, and oppression

Jon Voight, actor, starred in *Midnight Cowboy* and *Coming Home*

William Brugh Joy, new age doctor, proponent of balancing energy of the chakras through a refinement of the sense of touch

Walt Whitman, poet

Paul Gauguin, French post-impressionist painter

Barry Commoner, biologist, ecologist, co-founder of the Citizen's Party

J. T. Kruger, South Africa's Minister of Justic and Police

Albert Sabin, developed polio vaccine

August Wasserman, developed test for syphilis

Patricia Neal, actress, played in *Hud*; recovered from severe stroke

Stymie Beard, child actor of *The Little Rascals*; later worked in drug rehabilitation after shaking the habit himself

Neil Young, rock musician

Johnny Winter, singer and guitarist

Virginia Woolf, writer

Arthur Penn, film director, noted for *Little Big Man*

Anthony Armstrong Jones, commoner who married a princess

Mel Ferrer, actor, played Toulouse-Lautrec

Vic Morrow, actor in TV series *Combat*

Joyce Brothers, pop psychologist

Galt McDermott

James Groppi, anti-war cleric

Leonard Woodcock, labor leader

David Riesman, sociologist, author of *The Lonely Crowd*

Beatrice Webb, Fabian socialist

George Gallup, pollster

Louis Kelso, attorney

Louis Armstrong, jazz trumpeter

Beatrix Potter, author of children's stories, best-known for *Peter Rabbit*

Arthur Koestler, writer, author of *Darkness at Noon*

Nikola Tesla, inventor, genius; invented alternating current

Graham Greene, author

Richard Hofstadter, historian

Robert Oppenheimer, A-bomb physicist

Bobby Seale, Black Panther, social activist
Henry Steele Olcott, co-founder of Theosophical Society
Emmanuel Swedenborg, scientist, mystic, clairvoyant
C.E.O. Carter, astrologer
Joe Sorrentino, judge; juvenile rights advocate
Alexander Haig, Nixon aide, involved in Cambodia
  bombing, Chile coup

Chapter Eleven

Phase 8: The Actress

Gemini Phase: Of the nature of the Sun, Venus, and Mercury
Image: The first act of a romantic comedy: a beautiful woman, wearing a white evening dress and a diamond tiara, is descending a staircase into a garden. There she encounters her two suitors. One is a gardener, who kneels on one leg and offers her a flower. The other is a handsome but haughty aristocrat, who looks intently into the distance. The lady startles him with a witty remark.

During Phase 7, the individual was immersed in collective concerns. He was trying to free himself from "the sins of the father" by dedicating himself to the problems of his people. When the Moon passes the 90 degree mark, however, the "imposed mask" breaks away, and the individual is suddenly transfixed by an idealized image of himself. There is nothing ordinary about this new self-image; the practicality of the dark Taurus phases has been left behind and he has entered into the glassy brilliance and transparency of Gemini.

The Phase 8 personality is highly idealized, almost abstract. It borrows from the light of the Sun, the Moon, and the stars, and evokes all of life's fullest implications. It brings the idealized world, the fantasy world, into everyday life, and thus, raises everyday life to a higher plane. The magic of Phase 8 is the magic of the stage. It is the ability to get people's attention, to make them forget their individual realities and enter into one's own. The

Phase 8 individual is an actor at heart. He is always at work defining and redefining his personality, identifying with one personality trait and rejecting another, playing with the forces of light and shadow to create a mask that is fully believable. Since he loves the limelight, he will often channel his powerful ambition in the direction of public life. If the truth be told, he wants to rise like the Sun, becoming ever more visible to the world at large. He has a lot to say, and he'd like the world to listen.

Chronologically, Phase 8 is related to late adolescence, and the individual's first real attempts to enter into society. He is cultivating his appearance, his dress, and his manners, in order to become more popular. Much experimentation is going on here. Different masks are being tried on and different personality traits emphasized, as he attempts to find a combination that is comfortable and expressive, as well as popular with the public.

Since Phase 8 begins with a square between the Sun and Moon, there is a lot of tension here—tension between the inner and outer sides of the personality. The individual has a very exalted vision of himself. However, before he will be allowed to live into that vision, he must first translate it into a socially acceptable form. This is a difficult process, fraught with awkward and embarrassing moments. Through practice, however—practice and *repetition*—he can perfect the Mask until it no longer even seems like an act. But there is a danger: if he falls into the illusion completely he will become slick and plastic.

As a phase of early adulthood, the persona passes quickly from one of undifferentiated friendliness, to same-sex bonding, to sexual role-playing. In the development of the Mask, traits considered attractive and appropriate to one's sex are emphasized, while those considered inappropriate are de-emphasized and even repressed. At the same time, there are apt to be individualistic cross-overs, where some of the positive traits associated with the opposite sex are incorporated into the conscious persona. Negative cross-overs will find their way into the personality through subconscious behavior, or be expressed through one's choice of lovers.

In the image, the princess's two suitors—the aristocrat and the gardener—symbolize the basic polarities of Gemini: city vs. country, sophisticated vs. unsophisticated, rich vs. poor, mental vs. physical. The unsophisticated, but emotionally genuine country boy idolizes the princess, since she is totally unlike any of the women he has previously known. The aristocrat is incapable of such adoration. Because he comes from the same social class, he is able to see through the princess's glamorous clothes and refined behavior to the mere mortal within.

The way that one expresses oneself—haughty or humble, polished or crude, articulate or inarticulate—is a crucial factor in gaining entrance to any social group. To be socially effective, a person needs to be both flexible and astute, for what works in one situation can be disastrous in another. For instance the gardener, knowing that he is uneducated, can still use his innocence and country charm to win the heart of the princess. At the same time, he must be sensitive enough to her sensibilities to know what will pass as charming and what seems merely crude.

Looking at the image on a more abstract level, we can see the gardener as the body, the aristocrat as the perceptual intellect, and the princess as the soul, mediating between them. The soul is being asked to choose between the intellect and the body, between Platonic and sexual love. Since this is an impossible decision, a romantic triangle emerges, which if properly handled, allows the princess to put off her decision indefinitely.

At Phase 8, and the waxing square between the Sun and Moon, the individual moves from a predominantly solar consciousness to a predominantly lunar consciousness. He moves from the world of spirit to the world of form. The sad part of this is that he is leaving behind the innocence and simplicity of childhood, and entering into all the artifice and complications of adult life. But the phase also has its happy side, for he is being intitiated into a brand new life—of courtship, sexuality, ambition, and independence. He has become his own person.

Phase 8 Examples

Paulette Goddard, actress in Charlie Chaplin films
Ruby Keeler, actress and dancer
Vivien Leigh, actress, Scarlett O'Hara in *Gone With the Wind*
Mary Astor, actress, played in *The Maltese Falcon*
Florenz Ziegfield, Ziegfield Follies
Fanny Brice, comedienne, Ziegfield Follies
Barbara Streisand, singer, actress, played Fanny Brice in *Funny Girl*
Liza Minelli, singer, actress, played in *Cabaret* and *Arthur*
Scott Joplin, ragtime composer

Jack Benny, comedian
Bela Lugosi, actor, best known for his vampire role
Mickey Mantle, baseball slugger
Steve Reeves, actor in *Hercules* movies
Bud Abbott, of Abbott and Costello comedy team
Robert Louis Stevenson, writer, author of *Treasure Island*
Charles Schulz, cartoonist, creator of "Peanuts"
William Kunstler, radical lawyer, defended the Chicago Seven
Erica Jong, author of *The Fear of Flying* and *Fanny*
Richard Wright, author, wrote *Black Boy*
Ronald Reagan, actor and U. S. President
John F. Kennedy, U. S. President
Alex Haley, author of *Roots*
Kreskin, stage magician
Jim Bailey, female impersonator
Bella Abzug, radical politician, feminist
Dylan Thomas, poet
Walter Cronkite, TV journalist
Edmond Rostand, author of *Cyrano de Bergerac*
Edward "Kookie" Byrnes, former youth idol, TV actor
Adelle Davis, nutritionist
Alice Bailey, occultist, Theosophist
Jackson Pollack, abstract artist
Antonio Gaudi, surrealist architect
Rene Magritte, surrealist artist
Georges Seurat, pointillist artist
Marcel Duchamp, cubist artist, best known for "Nude Descending a Staircase"
Marshall Nirenberg, decoded DNA helix
Paul Guggenheim, art patron, founded the Guggenheim Museum
Joseph Campbell, mythologist, sage
T. E. Lawrence, Lawrence of Arabia
Ray Bradbury, science fiction author, wrote *The Martian Chronicles*

Chapter Twelve

Phase 9: The Gathering of Friends

First Cancer Phase: Of the nature of the Moon and Jupiter
Image: A group of friends sitting on a riverbank, watching a boat go by; a beautiful girl is playing the guitar.

After the personal struggles of Phase 8, the Phase 9 individual can now relax and ease back into the familiar rhythms of everyday life. She has no further interest in the grandiose self-image developed in Phase 8, for her desire for fame has given way to a desire for love and a sense of belonging.

Seeking out a slower, quieter existence, the Phase 9 individual is now trying to recapture her feeling for the broad and sweeping flow of life around her. Through meditation and quiet reflection she re-attunes herself to the changing rhythms and harmonies of nature. A new level of understanding is blossoming in her soul; her eyes are opening to the lyrical inner beauty of nature, and to the quiet life of the human soul hidden beneath the superficial commotion of life. She is beginning to understand the interrelatedness and interdependence of life. She is coming to realize that all of us, with or without our knowledge, from the beginning to the end of our days, are contained and sustained by the warm embrace of nature. She sees life stretching before her and behind her as an endless river which gives without measure, yet is always replenished. Thinking back to the common origin of all living things, her heart melts like ice in water. The human differences which seemed so important in Phase 8 now seem superficial and even quaint, for she finds that even differences of

IMAGE: PHASE 9

race, culture and nationality will begin to dissolve as soon as one begins to relate on the level of universal human emotions.

The soul-power of the Moon is at its height in this phase. The Phase 9 individual perceives the world with the eyes of the soul; her heart goes out to life. Emotionally susceptible, she has many moods, some of them lyrical and poetic, some strange and disquieting, some quite stormy. Because she is occasionally subjected to strong surges of emotion, one of her main concerns is in establishing an emotional center—a home base from which everything else in her life can derive its meaning. Much of her energy goes into exploring the feelings of her own heart. The instinctive understanding she finds there, the deep convictions welling up within, serve as reference points and stabilize her in her voyage through the uncertain waters of life. Thus while outwardly adaptable and sensitive to the changing moods of the environment, she is inwardly quite fixed, for she views absolutely everything within the context of her own internal value system. Anything that she can't internalize, anything that is truly alien, is either rejected or ignored.

Because of its relationship to the Moon, Phase 9 gives an extremely sociable and gregarious nature. The Phase 9 individual is often at the center of some little social scene, some cult or group bound together by an easy flow of emotion. Exuding warmth, tolerance and accessibility, she has a lot of popular appeal. She knows how to make people feel relaxed and comfortable, how to coax them out of their shells and get them to contribute to the scene. Her view of humanity is basically optimistic, because she has faith that the best side of people will emerge as soon as it is given a safe opportunity to do so. As a caring person, the Phase 9 individual takes responsibility for her immediate social environment. She is attentive to the quality of everyday interactions—to all those points of humor, aesthetics, or love that put meaning into life and lift it above the ordinary.

Starting from the heart, and from a sense of inner fullness, the Phase 9 individual expands her world to include her family, her intimates, her social circle, her town, her countrymen, her nation, and her world. While each of these levels has its boundaries—its little protective borders—each level flows fairly easily into the next. Thus, the Phase 9 individual is able to see the cosmic overtones of mundane events, the personal level of political life, the influence of social life on personal life, etc. Always, she acts to dissolve the boundaries between different levels of experience. She is humanizing, harmonizing, and drawing everything into the larger flow.

Phase 9 Examples

Odetta, singer
Lowell Thomas, TV commentator, actor in "High Adventure"
John Cameron Swayze, correspondent, known for "Sightseeing with the Swayzes"
Dave Garroway, talk show host
Joy Adamson, author of *Born Free*
Robert Young, actor in TV's "Father Knows Best"
Sanford Gottlieb, head of SANE, against nuclear weapons
Woody Herman, folk singer
Jonas Salk, developed polio vaccine; consciousness raiser among scientists
Linus Pauling, Nobel chemist; vitamin C proponent
Rembrandt van Rijn, Flemish painter
Bertrand Russell, philosopher, mathematician
Dorothy Parker, humorous writer for *The New Yorker*
Ralph Bunch, U. N. diplomat, educator
Floyd McKissick, Congress of Racial Equality head
Gary Snyder, poet, environmentalist
N. C. Wyeth, artist
Paul Badura Skoda, classical pianist
Maurice de Vlaminck, Fauve artist
Duilio Scandali, poet
Mark Twain, writer and humorist, author of *Huckleberry Finn*
Herman Melville, author of *Moby Dick*
Admiral Chester Nimitz, Pacific theater of World War II
Conrad Hilton, founder of Hilton Hotels
Vicki Baum, writer, author of *Grand Hotel*
Glenn Miller, Big Band leader in '30s and '40s
Benny Goodman, swing clarinetist, orchestra leader
Shirley MacLaine, actress, spiritual seeker
Arthur Freed, film producer of *The Wizard of Oz*
L. Frank Baum, author of Oz books (Phase 10?)
James Whitcomb Riley, the "Hoosier" poet
Mickey Rooney, actor, starred in "Andy Hardy" movies
Carl "Alfalfa" Switzer, child actor in *The Little Rascals*
Horatio Alger, author of "rags to riches" fiction
Bob Montana, author of "Archie" comics
Joyce Kilmer, poet, author of "Trees", died in World War I
Norman Vincent Peale, radio preacher, author of *The Power of Positive Thinking*
Grace Metalious, author of *Peyton Place*
Joni Mitchell, singer, composer

Chapter Thirteen

Phase 10: The Architect

Second Cancer Phase: Of the nature of Saturn and the Moon
Image: A brightly lit geodesic dome perched on an isolated hilltop, under a clear, starry sky. In the study, an architect is at work at the drawing board.

Eventually the individual tires of drifting along with the mainstream of humanity, for he is beginning to realize how unconscious they are, and how willingly they play out their lives in an empty fulfillment of social expectations and biological urges. Stepping back to collect his thoughts, the Phase 10 individual is further disappointed when he discovers how little effort people will make to understand him, and how quick they are to predict his behavior on the basis of his appearance or his social background. Unwilling to play into these games, he becomes extremely conservative in what he projects. He doesn't want people to assume anything; he wants them to ask.

Now that he is no longer tied to the consciousness of the masses, the Phase 10 individual begins to cultivate his mind in earnest. He haunts libraries and reads newspapers. Through practice he perfects his mental machinery and learns to process large quantities of mental data. Patterns begin to emerge, and soon he is constructing an ambitious theoretical framework by which to analyze reality.

Essentially his approach is conservative. Many of his opinions have been absorbed from his parents and his early childhood environment. While he will retain these ideas if they have served him well, he does not feel bound to them, and will probably outgrow them as time goes by. In his lifetime, he may shed a number of these intellectual "shells," as his worldview becomes ever more sophisticated and comprehensive.

If, however, he should become lazy, and stop entertaining new ideas, he soon becomes uncentered and maladapted. The outdated mental structure which he is imposing on reality actually begins to hinder the evolution of the people and institutions with which he is involved. Eventually his power to adapt to new situations rusts out completely, and he starts to mechanically repeat all of his old mistakes, like a robot missing a gear.

While the Phase 10 individual is something of an intellectual, he is also very practical; he would like his ideas to be put into effect. Concerned by the haphazard and incompetent organization of society, he will often work very hard to get into society's decision-making circles. For if society is to evolve to its highest form, its goals and values need to be consciously developed and competently administered. Society is like a body, and it should be organized like a body; the head should rule. When this is not the case, there are internal conflicts which result in a tremendous waste of energy.

In order to get an opportunity to materialize his ideas, the Phase 10 individual will have to achieve a position of some prominence and respect in society. This is often a lifelong process, involving a tremendous amount of discipline and personal effort. To make the road up the mountain surer and shorter, the individual constructs a long-range game plan, complete with intermediary way stations and detailed methods of procedure. But while these practical considerations are often vital to his success, it is even more important that he keep his spiritual goals constantly in mind, for it is easy to get lost in the complexities of the immediate situation, or to be tempted off the road by fame, money, status, or personal power. At best the Phase 10 person obtains only those things which he can give back to humanity. He seeks social power in order to build a better society, and spiritual and intellectual power in order to educate people and broaden their world-view. His highest ambition is to serve as a lighthouse to the public, illuminating their minds, dispelling their fears, and inspiring them towards conscious growth.

In Phase 10, the conscious ego is absorbing all that is dark and mysterious in the world and slowly transforming it into the light of conscious understanding. But the ego can only take on so much at one time. Thus, as it turns its attention to new fields of interest,

Figure 13.1

the older, more reliable elements of its mental system inevitably sink into the realms of the unconscious. There they stay until the memory is called upon to retrieve them and bring them back to center stage.

A similar pattern can be seen in biological evolution. Any newly-evolved faculty demands a considerable amount of conscious attention, but with time, the processes become routine, and are codified into instinct and memory. Nothing is ever really lost; it is just compressed and buried. Thus, in the developing embryo, all of the evolutionary forms of the distant past can be seen transforming one into another until the fetus begins to take on a distinctly human form.

Phase 10 Examples

    Carlos Castaneda, writer, *Don Juan* series
    R. D. Laing, psychologist, author of *The Politics of Experience*
    Isaac Asimov, scientist, prolific science fiction writer
    A. E. Waite, occultist, designer of the Rider-Waite tarot deck
    Guy Murchie, author, *The Music of the Spheres*
    Colin Wilson, writer, author of *The Occult, The Mind Parasites,* and *The Philosopher's Stone*
    Alan Arkin, actor, spiritual seeker
    Sri Aurobindo, spiritual teacher, community organizer
    Sir Arthur Evans, archaeologist, studied ancient Minoa
    Max Planck, scientist, developed theory of quantum mechanics
    Erich von Daniken, pop author of UFO books, wrote *Chariots of the Gods*
    Henry Kissinger, government advisor, former U. S. Secretary of State
    William Randolph Hearst, newspaper magnate

Dorothy Schiff, publisher of *New York Post*
Joseph E. Levine, movie mogul
Ella Grasso, ex-governor of Massachusetts
William C. Menninger, psychologist, founder of Menninger
    Foundation
Humphrey Bogart, actor, starred in *The Maltese Falcon* and
    Key Largo
Frank Rizzo, ex-mayor of Philadelphia
Earle Wheeler, member of U. S. Joint Chiefs of Staff
John Pierpont Morgan, financier
Brian Epstein, manager of The Beatles
Walt Rostow, political advisor of Lyndon B. Johnson
Paul Warnke, SALT negotiator
Claus von Stauffenberg, involved in plot to kill Hitler
Gerard Kuiper, astronomer
Tigran Petrosian, chess master
Martin Luther, leader of Protestant rebellion
Charles Darwin, theory of evolution (phase 9?)
Barbara Hepworth, sculptor
Hermann Buhl, mountaineer
Golda Meir, former president of Israel
Charles DeGaulle, general, former President of France
Joseph Esherick, architect
Edward Tolman, behavioral psychologist
Agnes Varda, director, known for "cinema verite"
Michael DeBakey, heart surgeon
Karl Ernst Krafft, cosmobiology founder; Nazi advisor

Chapter Fourteen

Phase 11: The Dream Wedding

Third Cancer Phase: Of the nature of Neptune, Venus, and the Moon
Image: A private wedding in front of a riverside cottage. The bride and groom exchange gold and silver rings under the rose-arbor, then thread their way through the cheering crowd to a little boat on the river.

The power of symbols has been growing steadily stronger since Phase 8, but with Phase 11 this process goes one step further. Here the individual leaves behind "objective reality" and enters fully into the dream—a dream that will remain coherent until Phase 16.

In Phase 11 the individual attempts to give birth to a romantic fantasy. She cherishes a luminous vision of the world as she would like it to be. In some ways this is a stock romantic vision: an idyllic home next to a rippling stream, shaded by swaying willows, with a happily married couple standing under the rose arbor, their children playing on the lawn, and larks flying joyfully overhead (tra la). Yet there can also be a strange surrealism to this vision, and curious twists and variations that touch reality in novel ways. The vision is somewhat artificial—embroidered by imagination and fantasy. But it also has a very real core, for it is based on a meditative attunement to the inner essence of nature.

By remaining open to the romantic possibilities in every situation, the Phase 11 individual hopes to find someone with whom to make her dream a reality. And while millions of people have similar ideas, there is certain passivity in this attitude that is unrealistic, a desire for a love as inevitable as the dawn, and just as easily attained. In the real world, relationships need someone at the helm to guide them over the reefs of emotional assumptions and psychological projections, to steer them away from dangerous currents, and to watch for obstacles in the river ahead.

The romantic and sexual aspects of the relationship also need to be cultivated—and if the relationship is to last, the romantic element must dominate. This is achieved through a kind of emotional enchantment—an active magic which uses sexual polarities to raise sexuality to a higher level of expression.

In the image, the boat represents the passage of the soul through life. It shows life as a emotional *balancing act,* where there is always a real danger of getting in over one's head. The voyage of the soul becomes safer once the individual has found a romantic partner, for the primal masculine and primal feminine find no balance until they have been united. Every relationship partakes of this union of the primal masculine and feminine. Thus, the subtle emotional adjustments that bring people into more intimate emotional union also represent—on a microcosmic level—the dawning of a more loving and harmonious world.

In the image, the newlyweds are establishing a new home alongside the river of *memory,* which pours the waters of the past into the future. To decorate their home, they gather together all those things that summon up the best memories of childhood. Stretching a silvery net across the river, they strain what is spiritually nourishing from what is spiritually inert. From the two piles two trees will grow. The first is the tree of life—the silvery sycamore—symbolizing spiritual recollection (or re-*collection).* The second is the tree of self-forgetfulness—the weeping willow—whose tangled roots reach deep into the muck of material existence.

In this dream landscape, there are also dangers. Near the willow dwells a water serpent, represented in the heavens by the constellation Hydra. Hydra symbolizes sexual memory, which can hypnotize the soul, and lead the individual into self-destructive activity. Other aspects of memory are equally problematic. Unconscious patterns of behavior inherited from her parents, or from past events, can make the Phase 11 individual unconsciously recreate unpleasant situations from her past. Therefore, at times she may find herself playing out unconscious scripts that seem more appropriate to a dream or a soap opera.

But this is all illusion, a bubble that is easily popped. Calling on her buoyant sense of humor, she need only shake the sleep out of her eyes, and take a new look at the problem. Once she has gotten in back of the situation, she will find it fairly easy to extricate herself from the emotional tangle she has unconsciously created.

At best, the Phase 11 individual lives in her dreams rather than her desires. She drifts over life's complications much as a boat drifts over the submerged roots of a tree. By allowing the chaotic patterns of everyday life to recede into the background of consciousness, she is able to direct her concentration to the inner world. With time, the swirling confusion of her Neptunian mysticism gives way to serenity and order, as the timeless ideals of the heart are condensed and fixated. A light pole is born within, which blossoms into the real world in the Leo phases that follow.

Phase 11 Examples

Ingrid Bergman, actress, starred in *Casablanca*

Sophia Loren, actress, starred in *Two Women*

Rudolf Valentino, silent film idol in *The Sheik*

Mary Pickford, silent film actress, known as "America's Sweetheart"

Dave Fleischer, artist of Betty Boop cartoons

Nino Rota, composed music for Fellini films

Jerome Kern, Broadway songwriter, author of "Smoke Gets in Your Eyes"

Busby Berkeley, extravagant Hollywood choreographer and set designer

Henry Mancini, composer, wrote film score for *The Pink Panther*

Henry Fonda, actor, starred in *The Grapes of Wrath*

Olivia Newton John, Australian pop singer, actress in *Xanadu*

Alain Delon, French actor, known for his gangster roles

Jean-Paul Leaud, French actor in Truffaut films

Patty McCormack, child actress, played in *The Bad Seed*

Terry Southern, comic writer, author of *Candy* and screenplays for *Dr. Strangelove* and *The Loved One*

Patrick Dennis, author, wrote *Auntie Mame*

Mary Wilson, singer, member of The Supremes

Doug McClure, actor in fantasy adventures

Tony Curtis, actor, starred in *Some Like It Hot, The Sweet Smell of Success*
Sally Field, actress, played in "The Flying Nun" TV series; progressed into Phase 12 with her film *Norma Rae*
Fernandel, French comic actor
Lyonel Feininger, artist
Man Ray, surreal artist and photographer
Henry Moore, abstract sculptor
Edmund Halley, astronomer, discovered Halley's comet
H. G. Wells, historian, novelist, wrote *The Time Machine*
Edith Hamilton, historian, author, wrote *The Greek Way*
Leonid Massine, ballet choreographer, acted in *The Red Shoes*
Anna Pavlova, ballerina
Ezio Pinza, opera singer
Danilova, ballerina
Paddy Chayevsky, playwright and screenwriter, whose credits include *Marty* and *Network* (10?)
Victor Borge, comic pianist
Nikita Khrushchev, Soviet leader, exposed crimes of Stalin era
Father Flanagan, founder of Boy's Town
Margaret Sanger, early advocate of birth control
Susan Brownmiller, feminist, wrote *Against Our Will*
Eugene Schoenfeld, called "Dr. Hippocrates," provided medical advice for hippies
W. A. Christiansen, founded organization for providing Seeing Eye Dogs
Franklin Roosevelt, U.S. President, author of New Deal policies
Farrah Fawcett, actress in TV series "Charlie's Angels"
Arnold Schwarzenegger, body builder and actor, starred in *Conan the Barbarian*

Chapter Fifteen

Phase 12: The Warrior King

First Leo Phase: Of the nature of Mars, Pluto, and Sun
Image: Tenth century England; a throne room hung with banners picturing rampant lions. The King warily confers with his astrologer, before re-entering the battle raging outside.

The Phase 12 individual realizes that he can't just depend on wishful thinking to get what he wants. He has to pursue his goals actively and aggressively, for in the real world it is the strong who prevail. Inevitably, cruder Phase 12 individuals resort to physical intimidation to get what they want, but even the most idealistic and non-violent members of the clan must be strong enough to stand up to physical force, for power relationships are an important part of life, and will not go away for being ignored.

The Phase 12 individual has large reserves of personal power, chiefly in the form of physical and sexual energy. Positively, he learns how to channel this energy towards noble goals. The image he embodies is heroic; he envisions himself as the proud king of the symbol, a champion of the light force, fighting with courage, sincerity, and unyielding determination to defeat the evils of the world and to establish a political order based on positive spiritual values.

Negatively, he feeds his energy into base desires, and his proud Leonine heart—with its inborn sense of goodness and divine purpose—is weakened and confused by doubt and shame. Unable

IMAGE: PHASE 12

to openly pursue his baser passions, he resorts to strategies, ploys, and deceit. And while he may become quite an expert at uncovering other people's games, he will have little success in attaining his own higher goals.

On a symbolic level, Phase 12's positive and negative sides can be seen as the lion and the snake: the noble-hearted regent and his wise, but evil advisor. While both of these aspects are always operating within the Phase 12 personality, one will always dominate, for the light force and the dark force are forever at war with one another. We find a similar relationship between the North and South Nodes of the astrological chart. If the North Node dominates, then the planetary energies of the chart are mobilized in a spiritually positive direction. If the South Node dominates, the energy flow is reversed, and spiritual and physical illness result.

There is also a relationship between Phase 12 and the kundalini energy: the serpent power at the base of the spine. In its primitive form the kundalini is the source of a hundred conflicting desires; it is a nest of serpents. But when it is mastered by a strong spiritual will, the kundalini rises up the spine and increases the individual's usable energy a hundred fold.

To accomplish this transformation, the individual must wrench attention away from the desires and fears of the subconscious, and turn his head towards the light of the future. Feeding on thoughts of spiritual victory, the "solar substance" of these thoughts gradually infuses his entire being, and lends him a sense of confidence and well-being. Thinking like a winner, he becomes a winner. Furthermore, since the conflicting desires of his lower nature are no longer given much thought, they lose a lot of their psychological power, and become malleable enough to be sublimated and interwoven into satisfying and productive behavior patterns.

In the intermediate stages of development, the Phase 12 individual will generally surround himself with images and props that cast a flattering reflection on his ego and his scene. While this can border on narcissism, there is really more to it than that. For if an individual is not personally controlling the imagery of his environment, he inevitably will be subjected to many images that are designed to erode his will and bring him under the spell of society's "dream masters." This is the secret of advertising and propaganda. Images may appear harmless, but they are really very powerful. They imply values, beliefs and directions. Thus, if a person wants to change the direction of society, he must first change its cultural imagery, and make that cultural imagery desirable.

The Phase 12 individual understands power. He knows who has it, how they got it, and what they are doing with it. While he has a clear understanding of society's dominant vision, he buys into very little of it. We often can find him as the central and sustaining figure of some subcultural or countercultural group. By establishing his own scene, and expanding his influence through that scene, he maintains a psychological advantage in his relationships with society. For instead of wasting his energy in a futile attack on society's monolithic illusions, he is able to draw his opponents onto his own ground. Unable to budge him from his position, their very efforts tend to give him attention and credibility. If the time is right, people will rally to his support, and it becomes entirely possible for him to emerge as a significant new force on the cultural-political horizon.

Phase 12 Examples

Napoleon Bonaparte, conqueror, self-made emperor of France
Ralph Nader, consumer advocate
Duong van Minh, "Big Minh," opponent of Thieu in Vietnam
Linda Jenness, Socialist Workers Party candidate
Oral Roberts, faith healer, TV evangelist
Rudyard Kipling, author, wrote *The Jungle Book, Captains Courageous*
Alfred Dreyfus, French army officer, victim of anti-Semitism
Catherine de Medici, instigator of St. Bartholomew's Night massacre of French Huguenots
Jesse Owens, runner, showed up Hitler at Munich Olympics
Dalton Trumbo, screenplay writer, blacklisted
Oliver Reed, English actor, starred in *The Devils*
Johannes Kepler, pioneer in astronomy, astrologer
Judy Blume, controversial children's book author, author of *Blubber*
Judy Collins, folk singer
Dick Gregory, comedian, peace activist, health advocate
Aleister Crowley, magician, poet
Alfred Noyes, poet, wrote "The Highwayman"
Elijah Mohammed, Black Muslim leader

Toshiro Mifune, actor, known for Japanese samurai roles

El Cordobes, bullfighter

Vladimir Nabokov, author, best known for *Lolita*

Ngaio Marsh, mystery writer

Harlan Ellison, science fiction writer

Thomas Wolfe, writer, author of *The Electric Kool-Aid Acid Test* and *The Right Stuff*

Linda Blair, actress, starred in *The Exorcist.*

Michelle Philipps, singer with The Mamas and Papas

Georges Clemenceau, general, led France through final phase of World War I

Akiro Kurosawa, film director of samurai films, noted for *The Seven Samurai*

Charles Steinmetz, physicist, dwarf, socialist

Lise Meitner, physicist

Babe Zaharias, early female golf pro, Olympic athlete

Roger Bannister, first runner to break four-minute mile

Tom Landry, football coach

Arthur Burns, ex-head of Federal Reserve Board

William Colby, ex-head of CIA

Edward Teller, Manhattan Project scientist, advocate of nuclear power

John Foster Dulles, Secretary of State under Eisenhower

George Carlin, comedian

Dionne Warwick, singer

F. Lee Bailey, controversial lawyer

Chapter Sixteen

Phase 13: The Dancer

Second Leo Phase: Of the nature of the Sun
Image: A beaming hula girl at a harvest luau, dancing beneath the sweltering Hawaiian Sun.

The inner passion of Phase 12 can no longer be contained or sublimated, so it explodes onto the scene in an exuberant display of creative energy. Phase 13 is ruled by the Sun in Leo, and these people are practically bursting with physical and mental energy. Warm, expressive, confident, sometimes arrogant, the Phase 13 individual combines great natural dignity with earthy approachability and humor. Her real strength, however, lies in her ability to live for the moment, to be herself and express herself at all times. She seems to be able to infuse life and drama into the most mundane situations—a quality that endears her tremendously to her associates. Encouraged by her big-heartedness and broad tolerance, the people around her eventually open up and express themselves. Not surprisingly, she often has a broad circle of friends, some of them going all the way back to childhood.

The Phase 13 individual has a special love for children, and usually wants to have some of her own. As a parent she is attentive, protective, and eager to share her wisdom and experience. Having never lost her own exuberance for life and her love of fun and play, she often finds it easier to express herself around children. Though she is extremely sensual, there is an almost child-like quality to her sexuality. She approaches sex imaginatively and passionately. She loves to seduce, to demand, to dress up, to play the role, but because she realizes that it is play she avoids getting stuck in any role that is too rigid or uncomfortable.

Negatively, the Phase 13 individual shows all the bad traits of the Leo; she is bossy, demanding, imperious and self-absorbed. Having forgotten the divine source of her own energies, she can find spiritual replenishment only in the devotion of others—and that is never enough.

The Sun has to do with the central purpose of manifestation, which is to give pleasure to God. The evolved Phase 13 is consciously aware of this purpose. She sets out to enjoy life purposefully. However, rather than selfishly hoarding her pleasure, she radiates it outwards towards the whole of creation, and thus participates in a greater -than -human pleasure. Each day her eyes are opened to new sources of enjoyment, as she slowly learns to see the creation as God sees it. She takes special delight in other people, for she is able to see beyond differences of race, age, sex, and personality to the original face of humanity—the human face first conceived in the mind of God. Recognizing the seed of divinity in her own talents and skills, she develops these talents not only as a source of personal pride and pleasure, but as a devotional offering for the amusement and delight of the Creator.

As the Phase 13 individual ages, she tends to grow more contemplative and philosophical. Her original belief in the goodness of life is solidified and strengthened, for everywhere she looks she see life's insatiable hunger for more life, life's desire to protect itself, enjoy itself, and propagate itself. Eventually the Phase 13 individual becomes something of a grand old man or grand old dame, surrounded by a wide circle of friends, family, children, and admirers—all eager to hear her stories and to bask in the warm radiance of her personality.

Phase 13 Examples

Janis Joplin, rock singer
Harry Truman, U. S. President
Sonny Jurgenson, quarterback, sportscaster
James Brown, soul singer
Chubby Checker, rock star, famous for "The Twist"
Milton Berle, comedian

Barbara Feldon, actress, starred in TV's "Get Smart"
Edith Piaf, chanteause
"Buffalo Bob" Smith, of TV's "The Howdy Doody Show"
Al Capp, cartoonist, creator of "Li'l Abner"
Daniel Moynihan, politician
Claire Booth Luce, politician
Miles Davis, composer and performer, jazz trumpet player
Norman Mailer, author, wrote *The Armies of the Night* and
  The Naked and the Dead
Hart Crane, poet
Ernest Hemingway, author, wrote *A Farewell to Arms* and *The
  Sun Also Rises* (phase 12?)
Cesare Pavese, author, wrote *The Moon and the Bonfire*
Simone Weill, writer, mystic
Sidney Greenstreet, actor, played in *The Maltese Falcon*
Peter Lorre, actor, starred in *The Maltese Falcon*
Pablo Casals, classical cellist, (phase 12?)
Joseph Szigeti, classical violinist
Jascha Heifetz, classical violinist
Andres Segovia, classical guitarist
Mstislav Rostropovich, classical cellist
Django Reinhardt, jazz guitarist
Artie Shaw, swing clarinetist
Perry Como, crooner
Annette Funicello, Mouseketeer, actress in beach party movies
Zero Mostel, comic actor, played in *The Producers*
Max Schulman, author, wrote *Dobie Gillis*
Roy Rogers, cowboy actor, fast food franchiser
Flip Wilson, comic
Rod Laver, tennis pro
Kyle Rote, soccer player
Hedda Hopper, gossip columnist
Mario Puzo, author, best known for *The Godfather*
Lili St. Cyr, stripper
Nelson Eddy, crooner
Tennessee Ernie Ford, singer
Jean-Paul Belmondo, actor, starred in Goddard's
  Breathless

Chapter Seventeen

Phase 14: The Vision Quest

Third Leo Phase: Of the nature of Mars, Jupiter, and Neptune
Image: A ragged soldier, still bloody from battle, climbs a desert mesa to survey his situation. As he nears the top he makes out a woman with long golden hair, looking down on him serenely. Behind her is a rainbow, which appears to have just touched down.

With the onset of Phase 14, the individual begins to catch glimpses of strange new truths that have no place in his old world view. Rather than ignoring these intuitions and rambling aimlessly through life, the Phase 14 individual leaves behind the myopic views of society and sets out on a solitary quest to discover how these new intuitions fit together. To succeed in this mission he will need all the determination and endurance he can muster. His will is going to be tested and tempered like steel. He will have to walk through the fires of war and the ice of winter, and yet remain unswayed from his inner course.

The shining goal which the Phase 14 individual has envisioned is really a symbol of his own higher self as it exists in a future state of completion. But until he has made considerable progress on his journey it is impossible for him to really know this. He is like a mountain climber who has taken a shortcut to the summit through a natural tunnel. At first he is just following a tiny light at the end of the tunnel, but when he reaches the top, that light expands into a panoramic vista, and he knows what it is he has been struggling for.

In the first part of his journey, the Phase 14 individual tends to project the missing components of his higher self onto external situations and events. He is always searching for some clue in the outer world that will awaken his own inner knowledge—a golden key that will unlock the door between what is and what could be. He is strongly attracted to people who seem to possess qualities that are as yet only latent in his own personality. By getting to know these people he hopes to incorporate some of these qualities and thus achieve a more balanced and integrated personality. Though this is basically a spiritual process, it is usually also sexual, since the missing qualities are often stronger in the opposite sex.

A complex inner alchemy is going on in Phase 14. The raw fire of sexual passion is allowed to burn freely when it is crowned by idealistic love. But when it becomes so hot that it leads to bondage and destructiveness, it is doused. The end result of this tempering process is the complete mastery of physical desires.

The individual becomes able to focus all of his desires on a single object, and to pursue that object with the full force of his being. Tremendous strides can be made once this has taken place, for his energy is no longer dissipated in side pursuits. As he begins to tap into the raw "sulfuric" energy that drives the first half of the lunar cycle, his reserves of physical energy become almost inexhaustible. The coarser part of this firey energy must be burned off physically, otherwise it will turn violent. But if he maintains and strengthens his ideals throughout this process, a transformation takes place whereby the coarser and cruder elements of the body are refined and spiritualized. The body becomes a golden chalice filled with light. It becomes so permeable to spiritual vibrations that he is able to know another's thoughts and feelings even from afar.

Despite all outward appearances, the main dynamic in Phase 14 is a progressive sublimation of sexual energy. Each stage of sublimation brings with it new powers, new opportunities, and new temptations. Phase 14 individuals are not really free to settle down in relationships until they have progressed into Phase 15, for as soon as they leave off their quest for "more realistic options," the entire process comes to a standstill. Sublimation must be a continuous and unbroken process, whereby the heavy lead of ignorance and complacency is transformed into the gold of self-knowledge, and the gold, in turn, is drawn out and refined into the light of spiritual wisdom.

In a sense, the vision which the Phase 14 individual is following is just an image, a shining "guardian angel" representing his own spiritual genius. But it can just as easily be said that it is really the body that is the image. One might say that the spirit is projected into the lower vibrational level of matter in order for it to grow spiritually; that the world is a testing ground wherein the spirit must strengthen itself, mastering the extremes in the environment and balancing the opposites within the personality. True, the Phase 14 individual must work to embody and flesh out his vision, but we must also remember that all of this activity is being guided by a consciousness that is entirely disembodied.

As the Phase 14 individual gets closer to his spiritual center, he begins to realize that all the experiences he has encountered in the "real" world were drawn to him as lessons in self-understanding and self-realization—that the world is an empty stage, a projection—given reality only by his hunger for experience; that the world is a desert except inasmuch as it provides opportunities for soul growth. He begins to see that all along the only solid thing was the immortal spiritual self, standing motionless at the outer periphery of the boiling cauldron of life.

Phase 14 Examples

Kirk Douglas, actor, played in *Spartacus* and *Paths of Glory*
Lewis B. Leakey, anthropologist, discoverer of early hominids
Ruth Benedict, anthropologist
Douglas McArthur, soldier, general in World War II and
Lord Horatio Kitchener, soldier in Sudan and Boer War
Erwin Rommel, German Field Marshal under Hitler, Afrika Corps
John Glenn, astronaut, politician
Robin Moore, author, wrote *The Green Berets* and *The French Connection*
James Joyce, author, wrote *Finnegan's Wake* and *Ulysses*
Country Joe McDonald, rock star, member of Country Joe and the Fish
Peter Max, 'psychedelic' artist
B. Traven, author, best-known for *Treasure of the Sierra Madre*
James Hilton, author, *Lost Horizon*
Carol Reed, film director, known for *The Third Man*
Miguel de Cervantes, author of *Don Quixote*

Sergei Prokofiev, composer of *Peter and the Wolf* and *Alexander Nevsky*

Dixy Lee Ray, marine biologist, member of Atomic Energy Commission

Euell Gibbons, naturalist, *In Search of the Wild Asparagus*

Barbara Walters, newswoman, interviewer

Harold Gray, cartoonist, creator of "Little Orphan Annie"

Philip Jose Farmer, science fiction author

Michael Crichton, science fiction author

Sarah Bernhardt, stage actress

George Byron, English Romantic poet and adventurer

Idries Shah, writer on the Sufis

Richard Dreyfuss, actor, starred in *Close Encounters of the Third Kind*

Eve Arden, actress on TV's "Our Miss Brooks"

Joan Davis, actress on TV's "I Married Joan"

Ricardo Montalban, actor on TV's "Fantasy Island"

Cleavon Little, actor in Mel Brooks' *Blazing Saddles*

Jack Kerouac, "beat" author, best known for *On the Road*

Edward Bellamy, socialist visionary, author of *Looking Backwards*

Herman Wouk, author, wrote *The Caine Mutiny*

Margaret Rutherford, actress in detective movies

Sri Chinmoy, guru, musician

Maya Angelou, author, wrote *I Know Why the Caged Bird Sings*

Lee Marvin, actor, starred in *The Dirty Dozen*

Luciano Pavarotti, operatic tenor

Thomas Hart Benton, American artist, created dreamy myths of American life

Charles Bronson, actor, starred in *Death Wish* and *The Great Escape*

Claudette Colbert, actress, starred in *It Happened One Night*

Chapter Eighteen

Phase 15: The Beloved

Virgo Phase: Of the nature of the Moon, Venus, and Mercury
Image: A winsome country girl leans gracefully against the pillar of a courthouse, and sniffs a wild rose. A diamond necklace hangs loosely from her back pocket.

At the exact full Moon the spirit seems to hover over the body, and for a moment we are able to see ourselves and the world with complete objectivity. Everything is revealed, for the physical body has become transparent to the soul within. Blind spots, defects of character, and unrealized potentials are all apparent, but on the whole it is a picture both beautiful and endearing. The spirit is finally able to accept its particular manifestation, and now marks it with its blessing. A new self-conception, and in particular a new body sense, is born of this vision, but it is still only a seed—a diamond in the rough—and after the vision has passed the individual must perfect herself as best she can. For though the relationship of spirit to body continues, it has lost its focus and clarity, so the soul must turn to its relationships with others for the experience it needs to grow and perfect itself.

The Phase 15 individual's main concern is with relationships. At the full Moon, the Moon seems to face the Sun directly. Similarly, the Phase 15 individual is refreshingly candid and direct in her relationships with others. She is always ready to draw other people into her intimate little world. Because of her vulnerability, her physical attractiveness, her engaging personality, her kindness and sensitivity, she is able to draw people out beyond their social roles, and get them to speak truthfully of their feelings and experience.

We also find an innate sense of sexual equality in Phase 15, based not on competition, but on a sense of the intrinsic worth of the individual. Actually, the more evolved individuals of Phase 15 exhibit a certain humility, for they look towards the highest in others, and thus bring their relationships to an exalted plane. In no other phase is it more true that we get what we give. The brittle egotism and vanity of the more negative examples never fail to draw a flurry of negative emotions from others. By contrast, the more positive examples exhibit an unspoiled naturalness that allows the beauty of the soul to shine through. Other people see in Phase 15 individuals more than has actually "come to earth," and this flattering reflection allows them enough psychological space to develop their better qualities.

On a less personal level, Phase 15 deals with the role of women in society. Thus in the symbol the courthouse represents the male-dominated society with its rules, its sense of values, and its vision of reality. The country girl, though presumably out of place, seems completely at ease. Independent of spirit, she is content with her own values and her own point of view. Though she is careless of society's artificial distinctions, she is aware of society's power, and uses her charm and social agility to stay within its good graces. Should it become necessary, however, she will not hesitate to override society's rules, even when this means a loss of social status. For just as the individual must adapt to the needs of society, society must adapt to the needs of the individual.

The strong social conscience found in Phase 15 individuals is rooted in a sense of balance and fairness, of give and take. Social reform is similarly perceived as a balance of creative and destructive forces. Thus, even as the Phase 15 individual attacks society's flaws, she is promoting a better vision of society and offering some practical ideas on how to make that vision a reality.

With the passage of the Moon through Phase 15, the individual gradually grows less dependent on society and other people for her self-definition. She has thought over her significant experiences and relationships, and reached many conclusions. Her analysis of the world has now become as tight and accurate as the bonds of a diamond. But more importantly, she has developed confidence in herself and her powers. She is no longer content to dodge society's games; she is ready to take on the world and set the rules herself. Excitement mounts as a new vision dawns—a vision of a social order based on honesty and love between people. Social agitation becomes the order of the day, as an infectious joy gets people to their feet and ready to participate in the dynamic social and spiritual movements of Phase 16.

Phase 15 Examples

Monica Vitti, Italian actress
Lily Tomlin, comedienne
Claudia Cardinale, Italian actress
Judy Garland, singer, actress, best known for *The Wizard of Oz*
Art Garfunkel, folk singer
Harpo Marx, comic actor
Edward Kennedy, U. S. senator
Charlie Chaplin, comic actor
Jerry Rubin, radical "hippy" in late 1960s, wrote *Do It*
Paul Goodman, author, wrote *Growing Up Absurd*
Jules Feiffer, intellectual cartoonist
A. S. Neill, radical educator, founder of Summerhill
Elizabeth Ashley, actress, played in *Ship of Fools*
Gertrude Stein, writer, author of *The Autobiography of Alice B. Toklas*
Elsie Wheeler, clairvoyant, channeled the Sabian symbols
Alice Hamilton, physician, industrial health advocate
Helena Rubinstein, cosmetics entrepreneur and businesswoman
Evangeline Adams, astrologer, defended astrology in court
Edith Cavell, nurse
Joseph Heller, writer, best known for *Catch 22*
Rachel Carson, environmentalist, writer, authored *Silent Spring*
Cat Stevens, singer
Carey McWilliams, editor of *The Nation*
William Carlos Williams, poet and physician
Ezra Pound, poet
Thornton Wilder, playwright, wrote *Our Town*
Gore Vidal, writer, critic, historian, author of *Julian* and *Lincoln*

Rene Girard, literary critic, author of *Deceit, Desire and the Novel*
Merce Cunningham, choreographer
Mikhail Baryshnikov, ballet dancer
Tom Bradley, mayor of Los Angeles
Sam Rayburn, famous Speaker of the House of Representatives
Louis Brandeis, Supreme Court Justice
Alfred Binet, psychologist, devised I.Q. tests
Thomas Morgan, geneticist, experimented with drosophila
Ernest Rutherford, physicist, pioneered studies in radioactivity
Juliette Low, founder of the Girl Scouts
Aimee Semple McPherson, evangelist
D. W. Griffith, filmmaker, known for *Birth of a Nation*
Gene Youngblood, film theorist
Beverly Sills, opera singer

Chapter Nineteen

Phase 16: The Procession

First Libra Phase: Of the nature of Jupiter, Saturn, and Venus
Image: In a windswept mountain pass, a huge, seated figure is being pulled over rolling logs by horses and crowds of straining men. The queen watches the distant spectacle from the royal rose garden.

As the Moon begins to wane a complete re-orientation of consciousness occurs. The soul's primary concern can no longer be found in the material world, for the drive towards incarnation has already passed with Phase 15. The opposite impulse has now come to the fore: the drive to merge with the Godhead. A powerful vision has awakened the soul—a vision of utopia, the cosmos, heaven, or the future—and the soul, straining to escape the restrictions of matter and form, seeks a quick and direct passage into these higher dimensions. Not content to merely glimpse the new reality through religious, artistic, or mythological symbolism, the Phase 16 individual attempts to enter fully into his vision, to live and breath it. But his visionary goal is still far away, so he must develop intense mental focus and concentration to keep from being side-tracked by more petty concerns.

Standing at a critical point in the cycle, the Phase 16 individual has an excellent perspective on the broader sweep of history, and often shows an interest in the history of civilization or the history of ideas. He takes a distant view of life, looking beyond

IMAGE: PHASE 16

particulars, to the intellectual, cultural, and spiritual forces that underlie all social progress. In reality, he tends to look at external events as mere symbols for the inner life of the spirit. His analysis is therefore aimed, not at factual accuracy, but at a clear exposition of essential truths.

The Phase 16 individual is able to perceive life from many different angles and viewpoints, appreciating each level of consciousness and how it fits into the evolutionary spiral. Furthermore, by understanding all the different "spokes in the wheel" he is able to intuit the dynamic center of the entire process, the ever-active creative point which we might call God. Spiritual memories of the past and presentiments of the future all serve to fan the flame of this primal spirit, but the closer the individual comes to center, the more irrational, frenzied, and formless the spirit becomes. Thus, if it is to be used for any broader social purpose the energy must be harnessed and channeled.

In the image, the wild horses of the spirit have been harnessed to pull a chariot, which symbolizes a religious or social organization. The monolith being pulled in the chariot can be a number of things, but in its highest sense it is a statue of the Buddha. Thus, the highest religions all promote meditation as the direct path to God-realization. Unfortunately, the vehicle of enlightenment—the religious organization—often becomes an end in itself, and the statue of Buddha, rather than serving as an exemplar of the perfected man, becomes an object of devotional worship. Instead of helping the individual in his spiritual growth, the organization may ride rough-shod over his spiritual individuality, turning him into a mere cog in the organizational machinery. Religious symbols are only keys; to open the door, we need to use them in meditative practice.

The problem of spiritual sclerosis is a constant one for the natives of this phase. In their youth they are generally discontented with old religious and social structures, battering them down furiously to make room for their burgeoning new realizations. Intoxicated by exciting new thoughts, dreams, mythologies, and visionary insights, their minds are chaotic and active. Living without structure is difficult, however, so they eventually tend to build up new structures of their own. Remaining open and clear-headed is their great challenge, for the highest approach to the primal spirit is to surrender to the energy and be carried along by it, entering into a blissful state which is both spiritual and sensual in nature. As sexuality is sublimated, an all-enveloping transpersonal sensuality blossoms. Their inner dreams, touched s o closely by the primal spirit, pour unchecked into the world, exciting and invigorating humanity with new vision and purpose.

Phase 16 Examples

Rudolf Steiner, philosopher, occultist
Immanuel Velikovsky, scientist (?), author of *Worlds in Collision*
William Blake, artist, poet, philosopher
Ernest Renan, historian, author of *Life of Jesus*
Paramhansa Yogananda, Indian spiritual leader (between 16 and 17)
Jeddu Krishnamurti, philosopher, renounced role as guru
James Van Allen, astrophysicist, for whom the "Van Allen" belt was named
Huey Long, populist demagogue
Leni Riefenstahl, Nazi filmmaker, known for *Triumph of the Will*
Guru Maharaj-ji, guru
F. Scott Fitzgerald, writer, author of *The Great Gatsby*
Elsa Maxwell, high society hostess
Alice Toklas, writer, companion of Gertrude Stein
Helen Hayes, actress
Julie Newmar, dancer
Anita Ekberg, actress, played in *La Dolce Vita*
Loretta Young, actress
Lauren Bacall, actress, starred in *To Have and Have Not,* and *Key Largo*
Glenda Jackson, actress, played in *A Touch of Class*
Rhonda Fleming, actress
Bing Crosby, crooner
Albert Finney, actor, played in *Tom Jones*
Percy Bysshe Shelley, Romantic poet
Groucho Marx, comedian
Paul Horn, flutist
Andrew Sarris, film critic
Eric Bentley, theater critic
Jerry TerHorst, press secretary for President Ford
Cecil B. DeMille, film director, best known for *The Ten Commandments*

Oliver Messiaen, composer
Edgar Snow, correspondent in China
Gladys Swarthout, opera star
Lina Cavalieri, opera star
Rennie Davis, political activist, member of the Chicago 7, later
a follower of Maharaj-ji
Viola Liuzzo, civil rights martyr
Johannes Brahms, composer
Andre Gide, unconventional writer and philosopher who had a
strong influence on French youth
Alexander the Great, military leader and conquerer, (birth data
questionable)
Al Hirt, trumpet player
Konrad Lorenz, animal behaviorist

Chapter Twenty

Phase 17: The Conjuror

Second Libra Phase: Of the nature of Pluto, Venus, and the Moon
Image: In an underground cave strewn with corpses, a giant satyr
lies sleeping. He wears a wreath of grape leaves, and is holding a
giant cup, from which wine is spilling. A muscular man is
escaping by shinnying up a rope through a hole in the roof. His
lover's face, framed by waving branches and brilliant sunlight,
looks down from above.

At the full Moon the soul became fully incarnated in the body. The
individual gained a whole-hearted belief in the objective, material
world and her own perceptual grasp of it. By Phase 17, this unity
of soul and body has begun to disintegrate. The soul's internal
image of the world is proving untrustworthy, awakening the
individual to the subjectivity of her own perceptions.

The teacher in this process is romantic passion. Open and
susceptible, the Phase 17 individual is quick to fall in love—for she
unconsciously projects components of her own soul onto other
people. Later, she may realize that the resemblance between her
lover and her inner ideal is largely an illusion, and the relationship
falls apart for lack of romantic and sexual tension. As this pattern
of disillusionment becomes unpleasantly familiar, the individual
realizes that she has been seeing essentially what she wants to see in
other people, and that the projective power of her subconscious is
rooted in her own desires. Her problem, then, is to is to be able to

discriminate between the subjective, emotionally-charged images conjured up by her subconscious, and the actual things they represent.

Psychologically, the Phase 17 individual stands at a balance point. She knows that she must eventually orient herself towards a more spiritual and ideal level of reality. However, it is difficult for her to relinquish her memories of the perfect union of soul and body that was experienced at Phase 15. An inner struggle results. On the one hand, she has learned that her own consciousness is the true agent in the construction of reality; she has discovered *psyche and symbol* as the keys to self-transformation. This often takes her into yoga, psychology, astrology, or magic. On the other hand, her psycho-sexual nature, like a sleeping serpent, does not want to be disturbed by these calls to evolution. It wraps itself up in fantasy and deceit in order to enjoy the sultry eroticism of its own dream world.

In the image we see a giant satyr wearing a wreath of grape leaves, and a overturned cup. The symbolism points to drunkenness, sexual excess, and the sleep of the higher mind that results from these stabs at Self-forgetfulness. The satyr may also be seen as a Libran symbol for the grape harvest—reminding us that there is a time to appreciate and enjoy the fruits of the year—a time for sex, revelry, and song. The overflowing cup of love was meant to be shared, for when it is not, the wellsprings of emotion become stagnant and corrupt.

The temptation to sexual excess is, however, strong, for this is a phase of great sexual charisma. To avoid falling into degrading behavior, either through personal inclination, or bad influences, the Phase 17 individual develops an personal code of behavior—a code of chivalry and restraint that helps her remain faithful to her romantic ideals and her higher self, and to walk confidently within their light. Should she fail in this, she will find herself spoiling her relationships through debaucheries that tarnish the image of her beloved, and her own image as well. Although a few excesses never hurt anyone, grave consequences will result if these excesses become habits, and lead to the corruption of her own spiritual self-image. For deprived of the central, luminous image of the soul, all the other images in the psyche will undergo corruption. The individual will be plagued by inner nightmares; she will inhabit a world crawling with decay, sleaziness, and deceit. Such an individual can become a danger to herself and to society, for she will be unable to separate the personal and impersonal elements in her fears.

Positively, the Phase 17 person is a romantic who brings the magical beauty of another realm into the lives of others, either through art or love. With time, she stops playing the field sexually, realizing that the image of divinity she is seeking in others cannot possibly be sustained in a prolonged relationship. She develops an increasingly personal and lyrical relationship with her own soul—her artistic muse—and this takes some of the pressure off her mate.

Yet there is always a note of melancholy here, for after autumn's ripe beauty, a period of darkness and corruption inevitably ensues. Common sense tells her to seize the day. Yet at the same time, fall's transcendant beauty reminds her that this world is only a dim reflection of more ideal plane of existence, a heavenly world of incorruptible love and beauty. This stings the soul with longing—unleashing an upsurge of emotion which seeks to break the bonds of everyday consciousness—to escape from the cave of inner darkness and her bondage to base desire. But as yet there can be no resolution to this problem; like the satyr, the Phase 17 individual is half-animal, half-goddess. There are moments of escape—of transcendant bliss, achieved through sex or romance, artistic rapture or drugs, but these are generally momentary. Afterwards, she sinks once more into her normal consciousness, or into those dangerous depths of illusion and fear that await the spiritually careless.

Phase 17 Examples

Walter Matthau, actor, known for his role in *The Odd Couple*
Robert Mitchum, actor, starred in *Farewell My lovely*
Sidney Poitier, actor, played in Lilies of the Field
Burt Reynolds, actor, starred in *Smokey and the Bandit*
Anthony Quinn, actor, played in *La Strada* and *Zorba the Greek*
Vince Edwards, actor, TV's "Ben Casey"
Francis Ford Coppola, director, best known for his films *Apocalypse Now* and *The Godfather*
Cher, singer, actress, played in *Silkwood* and *Moonstruck*
Angie Dickinson, actress, TV's "Police Woman"
Jean Genet, author of homo-erotic literature, wrote *The Balcony*
Bertolt Brecht, German playwright, author of *Threepenny Opera*

Lillian Hellman, writer, author of *Pentimento*
Stephen Crane, author, wrote *The Red Badge of Courage*
Yukio Mishima, decadent author, paramilitarist, died by hara kiri
Ursula LeGuin, science fiction , authored *The Lathe of Heaven* and T*he Left Hand of Darkness*
Jorge Luis Borges, surrealist author, wrote *Labyrinths*
Boris Spassky, chess master
George Washington Carver, scientist, known for his work with the peanut
Max Theiler, epidemiologist, developed vaccine for yellow fever
Charles Addams, cartoonist, "The Addams Family"
Ivan Albright, artist, did portraits of decay
Claes Oldenburg, sculptor, known for his oversized, soft sculptures of everyday items
Tomi Ungerer, humorous pornographic artist
Auguste Rodin, sculptor, best known for his works "The Kiss" and "The Thinker"
Mary Calderone, sex researcher, champion of birth control
Emma Goldman, anarchist revolutionary, champion of birth control and free love
Christine Jorgenson, transsexual
Christiaan Barnard, heart transplant doctor
Allen Dulles, set up CIA, was also on the Warren Commission
Dean Rusk, Secretary of State under Kennedy, ex-head of Rockefeller Foundation
Mao Tse Tung, Chinese communist leader
Ravi Shankar, sitarist
Gerard Croiset, psychic, noted for ability to find bodies
Amadeo Modigliani, painter
Warren Beatty, actor, director, starred in *Heaven Can Wait* and *Shampoo*
Theodore Roszak, cultural analyst
Noel Tyl, astrologer, opera singer
Tuli Kupferberg, singer for The Fugs
Eva Braun, mistress of Hitler
Kim Logan, past-life regression therapist, counselor for the dying

Chapter Twentyone

Phase 18: The Angel

Third Libra Phase: Of the nature of the Sun, Venus, and Pallas
Image: An angel, haloed by the Sun, hovering stiffly over a peaceful seaside suburb.

In Phase 17 outer forms decayed while inner forms became ever clearer and more refined. In Phase 18 this process of spiritual purification accelerates until a spiritual breakthrough occurs. The desire for illumination becomes stronger than the desire for worldly things; the desire to merge with the higher self becomes stronger than the desire to merge with the animal self. As the individual lets go of his desires, the spirit soars upwards onto a higher plane of consciousness. His head becomes clear and bright, his breath smooth and deep. He sees the world as if from far above. Everything is in perfect perspective, in absolute focus. There is a wonderful awareness of his place in the Whole, of his true spiritual identity—not the ego identity, which is based on personal needs and desires, but the true Self, the light of God which he carries within.

The Phase 18 individual has been resurrected from the grave of acquisitiveness and desire, and his eternal spirit housed within a temple of firm and unyielding character. Through attentiveness to his spiritual growth, the light of the self has been strengthened and fixated. He is now beyond the fear of death and the compulsions of the natural cycle. He stands above the whole, balanced between manifest and unmanifest, past, present, and future. While it is no longer necessary for him to participate in worldly affairs, a genuine spirit of helpfulness moves him to take an active role in human affairs. Since he is centered within himself and requires no support from the environment, he is not afraid to speak his mind—even when his ideas are unpopular. Confident in the invincibility of the truth, his words cut through the complexities of the situation like a ray of light in a darkened room.

The Phase 18 individual has a keen sense of history. Like the angel in the symbol, he stands at the periphery of the human drama, looking down with amused detachment, and offering help and advice where he can. He knows that the course of human evolution has been rocky, but he also knows that the light force and the power of peace have always prevailed in the end, for the light force has the overview, and is thus able to guide the course of events according to the will of the spirit.

On a mythological level, Phase 18 is related to Apollo and the Muses. The Phase 18 individual has a great appreciation for art, music, poetry, theater, dance, history, and philosophy. He is attracted to anything that cultivates and expresses the nobler qualities of the human soul. He is easily touched by human beauty, but also realizes that true physical beauty is an outward expression of the inner light of the soul. In relationships he looks towards the divine in others, and tries to give the higher self a place of honor, where it needn't get dragged into the petty problems of everyday life. His own respectfulness, attentiveness, and simplicity of feeling attracts similar treatment from others. Therefore, his relationships are often on a high plane—free, easy-going, creative, and marked by genuine caring. At best, he is capable of sustaining a truly spiritual marriage, in which the two partners love each other for the other's sake rather than for their own.

Phase 18 Examples

Flora Purim, jazz singer, known for "You Can Fly"
Jane Fonda, actress, political activist, exercise advocate
Lee Remick, actress
Greta Garbo, actress
Peggy Lee, singer
Argentinita, Spanish dancer

Ginger Rogers, dancer, actress, starred with Fred Astaire in *Top Hat* and *Shall We Dance*

Valerie Harper, TV actress

David Niven, actor, played in *Around the World in Eighty Days*

Jimmy Stewart, actor, starred in *It's a Wonderful Life* and *Mr. Smith Goes to Washington*

Dick York, actor in TV's "Bewitched"

William Bendix, actor in early TV's "Life of Riley"

Eddie "Rochester" Anderson, comic actor in "The Jack Benny Show"

Pat Boone, pop singer, evangelical Christian

Willie Mays, baseball star

Erma Bombeck, writer, humorist, wrote "At Wits End"

Yogi Berra, baseball catcher

Vilhjalmur Steffanson, Arctic explorer

Kenneth Murray, aviator

Le Corbusier, architect

James Barrie, writer, best known for *Peter Pan*

Jimmy van Heusen, songwriter, author of "High Hopes"

James Mitchener, novelist, wrote *Hawaii*

Irving Stone, novelist, wrote *The Agony and the Ecstasy*

I. F. Stone, radical journalist, historian

E. J. Hobsbawm, historian, author of *The Age of Revolution*

R. R. Palmer, historian, authored *A History of the Modern World*

Nat Hentoff, radical journalist

Phil Ochs, songwriter

Robert Frost, poet

William Butler Yeats, poet, occultist

Richard Alpert, guru, also known as Ram Dass

Alan Watts, seeker, popularizer of Buddhist studies

Stendhal, French novelist and essayist, wrote *The Red and the Black*

Jean Paul Sartre, existentialist writer and philosopher

Arturo Toscanini, orchestra conductor

Oliver Hardy, comedian

Madeline Kahn, comedienne, starred in *Young Frankenstein*

John Anderson, U. S. Senator, third party candidate for U. S. presidency

Chapter Twentytwo

Phase 19: The Wise Serpent

First Scorpio Phase: Of the nature of Pluto
Image: Raggle-taggle troupe of travelling actors perform a
medieval morality play; Eve and the serpent argue over the merits
of eating the forbidden fruit.

In Phase 18, the individual established a calm, clear, and expansive
overview of life; her consciousness spread over the world like the
rays of the Sun. But not everything is open to view; some things
are hidden—even purposely obscured. The Phase 19 individual
begins developing her consciousness within these dark areas. She
has a prying curiosity about all that is hidden and a desire to get to
the bottom of things, even when that means uncovering evil and
deceit. She knows that knowledge is power, and that this power
will allow her to mold the world according to her desires.
    While seeming to call everything into question, the Phase 19
individual is actually working on a system of her own—based on
those deeper glimpses of truth that sometimes pierce the world of
appearances. Realizing that true understanding relies not so much
on proper perception as on proper interpretation of perception, she
is constantly re-evaluating her experiences in the light of new facts
or theories. Every answer leads to a new question, as she pursues a
trail of clues, unraveling layer upon layer of ignorance and
misperception.

For the Phase 19 individual, Truth is like a snake crawling through tall grass; part is visible and part is hidden. Each of the five sense allows us to know reality in a different way, and together they imply a central reality. But do they all coincide? Or is there something wrong with the picture—some discrepancy that hints at misrepresentation or deceit? At this stage, it is often the *sixth sense* that points the way. However, even ESP and occult perception cannot be taken at face value, for they are channeled through the subconscious mind, and therefore, may be products of almost anybody's deluded consciousness—living or dead.

Phase 19 people generally have a good understanding of the political process, especially its internal workings—the political in-groups, the power brokers, the bartering of favors. But power has many levels. Often the most powerful politicians are spokespeople for particular philosophies or points of view. By aligning themselves with transpersonal forces, they are able to assume lead roles in the historical drama. In fact, they are convincing, they have charisma, to the very degree that they embody these principles.

In a way these politicians are just standard-bearers for the party intellectuals and policy makers. This inner circle of theoreticians is governed, in turn, by a spiritual leadership—either living or dead—which is the source of their entire world view. *This* is the level at which the most highly evolved Phase 19s are operating—the metaphysical, occult, symbolic level. Like the worm that crawls to the center of the apple, they crawl to the center of the dominant world view and eat away. Like skilled lawyers, they draw the priests and intellectuals into a verbal battle, where their real motives and suppositions can come to light.

In personal relationships, the Phase 19 individual is extremely generous—at least to those within her group. However, she defines this group rather narrowly, and guards its inner and outer boundaries with the vigilance of a watchdog. She tends to view other people in terms of their spiritual, intellectual, political, social, or financial power. These things are not valued for themselves, but are seen as resources for the advancement of her inner circle, or for the advancement of its *group consciousness*. Individuality *per se* is not respected; people are psychologically analyzed in terms of their ruling desires and ruling fears, not in order to manipulate them, but in order to understand the limitations of their viewpoints. For be it fear, or greed, or lust, or ambition, ruling passions are always the source of distortions and blind spots. As for controlling people, the Phase 19 individual is more likely to resort to emotional and intellectual browbeating, or to her uncanny way with words.

In the image, Eve is involved in a battle of wits with the serpent. She knows that he has some extraordinary perceptual power, but is wary about binding herself to him in order to get it. Through argument she tries to weaken his position, hoping to arrive at some acceptable bargain.

The same symbolism is repeated in the story of Pluto and Persephone. Persephone was exiled to the underworld for having eaten six pomegranite seeds. Symbolically, this shows the immortal soul being forced to incarnate because of its desires—to leave behind the flowery meadows of heaven for the bondage of earthly existence. The world is viewed as the underworld here, because at this point in the cycle, the light force is waning, and becoming subjugated to worldly forces like money and political power. The symbolism also refers to the fact that the soul, in taking a physical body, loses the larger share of its potentials, and is limited to the expression of one facet of its internal nature.

On a metaphysical level, Eve represents the waters from which the Creation emerged. The Egyptians referred to this as the Nun; the Hindus call it Prakriti. The gnostics call it Sophia, who created an *imperfect* reflection of the Godhead that eventually became our world. The "first matter" is virginal because it precedes all forms; it is fertile because it is the mother of all forms. On a personal level, it is the source of the immortal soul, from which all incarnations radiate, like the seeds of a pomegranite.

Phase 19 Examples

Arthur Conan Doyle, author, wrote the Sherlock Holmes series
Jim Garrison, District Attorney, investigated John F. Kennedy
  assassination
Daniel Ellsberg, exposed the "Pentagon Papers"
Clarence Darrow, lawyer, known for his role in the "Monkey
  Trial"
Carl Bernstein, reporter, cracked Watergate
Robert Woodward, reporter, cracked Watergate
Sam Ervin, directed Watergate committee
Leon Jaworski, prosecutor in Watergate hearings
John Dean, key witness in Watergate hearings

Erle Stanley Gardner, wrote Perry Mason stories
Alfred Kinsey, sexual researcher
Jerry Garcia, rock singer, cult figure, member of The Grateful
  Dead
Agnes Moorehead, actress, Endora in TV's "Bewitched"
Elizabeth Montgomery, actress, starred in TV's "Bewitched"
Alan Leo, astrologer
Boris Pasternak, author, wrote *Dr. Zhivago*
John C. Lilly, researched LSD, studied communication with
  dolphins
Buckminster Fuller, architect, proponent of geodesic domes
Samuel Beckett, absurdist playwright, author of *Waiting for
  Godot*
Cab Calloway, jazz singer
Michael McClure, author of "beast" poetry
Adolf Hitler, Nazi dictator
Cyd Charisse, dancer, actress, played in *Singing in the Rain*
Niccolo Machiavelli, early 'realist' in political theory, wrote
  The Prince
Joe Pool, member of the House Un-American Activities
  Committee
Arthur Rackham, illustrator
Marlene Dietrich, actress, played in *The Blue Angel*
George Harrison, musician, member of The Beatles
Meher Baba, guru, took vow of silence
Redd Foxx, comedian
Theodore Roosevelt, U. S. president, conservationist
Robert Penn Warren, writer, author of *All the King's Men*
William Styron, writer, author of *Confessions of Nat Turner*
C. V. Woodward, historian, wrote *Tom Watson: Agrarian
  Rebel*
Edward Albee, playwright, author of *Who's Afraid of Virginia
  Woolf?*
Connie Francis, singer and actress
Ellen Corby, actress, grandma in TV's "The Waltons"
Ken Kesey, leader of the Merry Pranksters, early LSD
  proponents; also author of *One Flew Over the Cuckoo's Nest*
Ornette Coleman, jazz saxophonist
Eric Hoffer, sociologist, longshoreman, wrote *The True
  Believer*

Chapter Twentythree

Phase 20: The Forgiven Heart

Second Scorpio Phase: Of the nature of Neptune, Mars, and Venus
Image: A young woman stands on a cliff by the sea; she carelessly
drops a flower over the side of the cliff. Behind her a black dog
rummages through a pile of garbage.

In Phase 19 the occult personality was uncovered and pieced
together. But this was largely an intellectual synthesis, and of
necessity it had many loose ends. In Phase 20, there is a desire to
reclaim the emotional center, to re-establish an intimacy with
nature and the life force. The main problem is karmic clutter—too
many thoughts, too many memories, too many mundane
complications in life, and not enough room to open up and feel.

    Phase 20 represents the end of an entire phase of soul growth. It
is a point of reappraisal and renewal, where the individual catches
his breath, and poignantly recalls the real reasons for his existence.
The Phase 20 individual knows of the divine beauty shining in his
soul. But he is also aware that there is a lot of trivial, ugly garbage
dragging him down and keeping him from evolving. At best, he
faces these problems squarely and makes an honest attempt to
extricate himself from the confining conditions and perceptions of
the past. In his reflections, he might be compared to a dog
rummaging through a garbage pile, for he must use discrimination
to sniff out the essential from the trivial. A lot of purging is taking
place here, especially on the emotional and sexual level, where

IMAGE: PHASE 20

jealousy, resentment, and selfishness must be acknowledged and washed away in gentle forgiveness. This is a long process, punctuated by intense personal crises, but the rewards are high, for the individual is attempting to uncover his true Self, and to reclaim his destiny from the control of extraneous forces.

Through his attentiveness to his own problems, the Phase 20 individual becomes more understanding of human problems in general. He can often be found teaching others constructive ways to approach and deal with their problems. Though generally gentle and warm-hearted, he can lapse into brutal sarcasm when nothing else seems to get through. Not surprisingly, this type of behavior becomes common when he himself is stuck in self-delusions or frustrating situations.

The evolved individual of this phase has very good insight into the complexities of the human condition. He sees the soul stretched uncomfortably between the conflicting demands of the spirit and the body. He sees the effects of the cultural environment on the way we think and feel. He sees how interconnected we all are, how one person's salvation is dependent on the salvation of the race. He sees how even the smallest of acts has its effects, and can tip the balance towards life or death. Thus, the rubbish heap in the symbol shows how acts of carelessness can accumulate and turn the world into an ugly place.

Love is not careless, for if a person really loves, he is careful and thoughtful about everything. He doesn't care for one thing at the expense of another. Love is not self-centered and blind. In its essence it demands a surrender of the ego, a willingness to let go. This surrender is symbolized by the flower falling into the ocean. Similarly, when the individual really lets go, he realizes that we are all only drops in the ocean. It is at this very moment, however, that he also recovers his sense of belonging. He remembers how to *feel* with nature and allow the life force to operate in and through him. Much pain and disillusionment accompany this sensitivity, for to be open to beauty his heart must be exposed. He must suffer rejection, betrayal, unrequited love, the death of those he loves. This is the wound of Christ, the bleeding heart surrounded by the crown of thorns. Here life and love are so intense they verge on pain. Yet in this pain there is also transcendance and regeneration, a healing spring of transpersonal love, which sustains the entire Universe, though few have eyes to see it.

Phase 20 Examples

Andy Griffith, TV actor
Don Knotts, actor on TV's "Andy Griffith Show"
Marilyn Monroe, actress, starred in *Some Like it Hot* and *The Misfits*
Gene Wilder, actor, played in *Young Frankenstein*
Arlo Guthrie, folk singer
O. J. Simpson, football star, running back
Dale Evans, TV actress, played in "The Roy Rogers Show"
Tony Randall, TV actor, starred in "The Odd Couple"
Harry Nilsson, rock singer
Brigitte Bardot, actress, environmentalist
Peter Sellers, comic actor, best known for his role in the *Pink Panther* films
Peter Falk, actor on TV's "Colombo"
Ramsey Clark, Attorney General under Lyndon B. Johnson, went on peace missions to North Vietnam and Iran
John Kenneth Galbraith, liberal economist
Maurice Sendak, author of children's books, wrote *Where the Wild Things Are*
Kurt Vonnegut, author, wrote *Welcome to the Monkey House*
Gunter Grass, author, wrote *Dog Years*
Hermann Hesse, author, wrote *Steppenwolf* and *Demian*
T. S. Eliot, poet, best known for *The Wasteland*
Dr. John, New Orleans rock musician
Patty Duke, actress, played Helen Keller in *The Miracle Worker*
Helen Keller, overcame multiple handicaps, socialist activist
Harrison Salisbury, correspondent, expert on Russia
Robert Burton, writer, author of *Anatomy of Melancholy*
Jane Addams, social worker
Staughton Lynd, pacifist
David Shoup, USMC Commander against the Vietnam War
Frances Willard, organizer of temperance movement
Maria Von Trapp, on whom *The Sound of Music* was based
Ottorino Respighi, modern "classical" composer
Vincent Van Gogh, post-impressionist artist
Edouard Manet, pioneer impressionist painter
Jean Sibelius, composer
Vaslav Nijinsky, ballet dancer
Richard Wagner, operatic composer
Frank Howard, baseball star

Billy Kilmer, football quarterback
Charles Atlas, body builder
Jayne Meadows, actress
Oswald Spengler, historian, authored *The Decline of the West*

Chapter Twentyfour

Phase 21: The Besieged Cathedral

Third Scorpio Phase: Of the nature of Mars, Moon, and Uranus
Image: A gothic cathedral besieged by a foreign army. The central tower has lost its roof and is now open to the starry sky. One of the rose windows has also been broken—close to its central Eye of God.

In the image, the cathedral represents a unified but highly complex mental system, which attempts to bring all truth within its compass. This synthesis is as much religious as it is rational and scientific; it seeks to impose a unified meaning onto all worldly events by placing them within an over-arching cosmological or metaphysical framework. On a cultural level, such a synthesis has not existed since the high Middle Ages, when St. Thomas Aquinas integrated Catholic theology into Aristotelian logic. The image takes us back to this period—to the cathedrals and cathedral schools, and the great European universities that were their offspring.

Inspecting the image more closely, the church can be seen as a symbol for the structure of civilization, with each story representing the work of a different generation. The rose windows, placed one above the other, represent the dominant world view or *cultural mandala* for each successive generation. Pictured in each rose window are the dominant religious and cultural myths around which society and its institutions are centered. By analyzing the position and relationships of these images one can determine the relative importance and interrelationships of the dominant myths. The rose window is like an eye within the eye, for it controls the way we organize and evaluate our perceptions and experiences. To change society, Phase 21 individuals must battle it out on this inner level. But to be effective, they must first have a grasp of society's present system of thought.

Though the Phase 21 individual generally begins her thinking along fairly traditional lines, it is not long before she is spotting contradictions and omissions. Eventually she starts building a system of her own, based on a modification of the old one. Through aggressive analysis and synthesis she eventually surpasses her society's old way of seeing things. However, if this synthesis is to be anything more than a construct, it must be fused at some point by a direct spiritual illumination. Much like the beam of light that shatters the rose window in the symbol, this revelation will usually outmode the old system of thought, parts of which will fall away, having been proven false. Understandably, there will be people in society who will forcibly resist these new ways of seeing things, particularly when they impinge on the society's central myths and beliefs. However, it is absolutely essential for the Phase 21 individual to enter into the social dialogue, and try to get her ideas across. What is at stake is the spiritual integrity and vitality of her society, for if a society stops integrating new ideas, new visions, and new perspectives, its rigid structure will eventually suffer a major collapse. With the collapse of its world view, the once-integrated society will splinter into a dozen warring factions, each with some fragmentary glimpse of the truth. Political and social disintegration may soon follow.

One might compare the Phase 21 individual to a Jewish physician, summoned to the court of an ailing Arab potentate. He is being called strictly in his role as a doctor. The fact that he is Jewish, that he is a Cabalist, is at best ignored. He must, therefore, bring all that he has to offer—his personality, his beliefs, his scientific and political insights—through his role as a *doctor*. At the same time, he must outwardly conform to the social expectations of an essentially alien culture. It is an uncomfortable position, and one that is apt to make him appear wooden and unnatural, if not downright deceitful.

Because the Phase 21 individual does not completely share the mythical assumptions of the dominant culture, she has a radically different *slant* on life. What seems perfectly acceptable to others may appear irrational and contradictory. At the same time, she may also see meaningful patterns where others see only confusion. She is thus in a unique position to offer solutions to society's ills, or to bind the dark forces of chaos with the subtle chains of reason.

Although the Phase 21 individual would like to restructure society according to her analysis, this isn't really possible, for her system of thought is far too complex and individualized to be easily assimilated. She refuses, however, to succumb to alienation, and waits instead for some window of opportunity to be opened to her. She wants and needs to belong, and will quickly rise to the occasion should society find some use for her talents. Often her contribution will be minor—some fragment of her thought will be used as a stone in the larger intellectual edifice; or, perhaps she will serve as a soldier protecting her country. At other times she may take the lead, using her superior analysis of society, of history, of human nature, to fashion a coherent social program or campaign that will lead society beyond its inner and outer strife to a new and higher level of integration.

Phase 21 Examples:

Jerzy Kosinski, novelist, wrote *The Painted Bird*, about wartime Poland

Winston Churchill, British Prime Minister in World War II

David Lean, filmmaker, known for *Dr. Zhivago* and *Lawrence of Arabia*

C. Eric Lincoln, sociologist, author of *Black Muslims in America*

Carl Rowan, political analyst

Francisco Serpico, policeman, exposed corruption in NYPD

Alexander King, writer, author of *Mine Enemy Grows Older*

Theodora Kroeber, anthropologist, wrote *Ishi in Two Worlds*

Albert Einstein, physicist, formulated the theory of relativity

Robert Wise, film director, known for *The Day the Earth Stood Still*

Josef Hynek, UFO researcher

Yul Brynner, actor, starred in *The King and I* and *Solomon and Sheba*

Anwar Sadat, president of Egypt, Nobel Peace Prize winner

Donald Menzel, solar eclipse scientist

Nicholas Copernicus, credited with formulating the heliocentric theory of astronomy

Tycho Brahe, astronomer, astrologer
Peter Hurkos, noted for doing psychic photography
Elizabeth Taylor, actress, starred in *Cleopatra* (Phase 20?)
Joan of Arc, saint and national heroine
Rick Wakeman, keyboard artist, known for "The Seven Wives of Henry VIII"
Edith Head, Hollywood costumier
Max Ernst, surrealist artist
Leslie Uggams, singer
Paul Simon, singer, songwriter
William Masters, sex researcher
Wilhelm Reich, sexual psychologist, founder of orgone theory
Erich Fromm, depth psychologist, wrote *Escape from Freedom*
Luis Bunuel, film director, made *L'Age D'Or* and *Viridiana*
Minoru Yamasaki, modern architect, Japanese Gothic in white stone
Robert Heilbroner, economist, author of *The Worldly Philosophers*
Jules Verne, writer, author of *20,000 Leagues Under the Sea*
de Nouy, philosopher, authored *Human Destiny*
Elizabeth Gurley Flynn, communist labor organizer
Elizabeth Kenny, nurse, polio researcher
William Peers, Lt. Calley's prosecutor
Mother Teresa, nurse, renunciant, received Nobel Peace Prize
Veronica Lake, vamp actress
Cliff Robertson, actor, played in *PT 109* and *Washington: Behind Closed Doors*
Ignaz Paderewski, pianist
Balanchine, classical ballet
Arthur Janov, psychologist, known for primal scream therapy
Henry VIII, king of England, broke with the Catholic Church

Chapter Twentyfive

Phase 22: The Carnival

Sagittarius Phase: Of the nature of Jupiter
Image: A Chinese sage walks calmly through a fairground. He passes a brightly lit ferris wheel, a hoochy-coochy dancer, and a fakir walking down a winding path of hot coals.

The battles of Phase 21 have left the individual feeling hopeless and paralyzed, but in a shattering intuitive insight he suddenly realizes that the mental system he has been building is hopelessly abstract and out of touch with reality. Detaching himself from the intellect's manic attempt to achieve immortality, he now relaxes, and loosens his grip on the "noble truths" he had sought to protect. The intellectual ego begins to fall away, and the individual slowly reawakens to the world outside himself. Amazingly, he finds it to be the same wonderful, expansive, mysterious world he had known as a child. He has made a long trip to be arriving back at the same place, but the fact is that his natural attunement to life had been drowned out by excessive intellectual "noise." At this point he is just remembering where he has always been.

By Phase 22 the intellect can no longer be trusted. It is too limited, too personal, too self-serving. It has become a con-man, a teller of tales. In order to re-attune himself to life, the Phase 22 individual must now develop his intuition, for intuition alone can illuminate and dispel the thousands of lies and half-truths deposited in the group mind by the intellect. Intuition is akin to feeling, and in that sense it is subjective, but it can give such an inclusive, subtle and penetrating understanding of one's situation, that it actually represents quite an advance over the intellect. Intellect, after all, is directed by personal desire, whereas intuition is passive and reflective; intuition subordinates itself to what *is*.

In order to develop his intuition, the Phase 22 individual must constantly exercise and test it in the environment. Every idea or impulse that comes into his mind must be projected outwards in thought or action. From the feedback he receives, he can judge the validity of his original assumptions, and work to further develop and refine them. Eventually he learns to trust his intuition to such a degree that he feels quite safe undertaking projects that others might consider extreme long shots.

As the Phase 22 individual develops a more comprehensive world view, other people begin to appear increasingly unconscious to him, for they are orienting themselves around unexamined myths and beliefs that insulate them from reality. Having no real center, no real self-awareness, they are unable to differentiate internal from external, symbolic from real. They are living in a dream world.

The Phase 22 individual is careful not to lose himself in the illusions of an unconscious society, so he generally takes very little at face value. Even when he gets swept up in the "carnival of life," there is always a part of him that is watching with amused detachment from a higher, more central perspective. This is not to say that he has the whole picture. Actually, there are so many holes in his conception of reality, so many absurdities, that he no longer really cares if he misses a few beats, or makes a few bad judgments. It is the living and the growing that really count, and the courage to follow his own truth wherever it leads. The Phase 22 individual is an active, reckless, participant in life. He doesn't just expound the truth; he lives it.

To the Phase 22 individual everything is mind, consciousness, energy. Only the self is solid; the rest is swirling illusion, a dance of divine energies, angels and devils, creative and destructive forces. Even so, the Phase 22 person does not reject the world, for it is through his relationships with the world and with other people that he is able to develop his higher consciousness.

The Phase 22 individual is an active participant in the mental and spiritual life of his society. He is a philosopher, a thinker, an innovator, a person who punctures outworn myths and promotes new ones. Through his intuitive understanding of the group mind, he is able to predict just which lines of thought will be effective in promoting the growth of human consciousness. He is relevant and timely, and often very funny. Sometimes he deals in pure philosophy, sometimes in pure fantasy, and often in a mixture of the two. He tries to make his ideas appealing, for while he wants to be truthful, he also wants to be effective. He wants to make a cultural impact.

Phase 22 Examples

Alan Ginsberg, "beat" poet, wrote *Howl*

Ruth Gordon, actress, starred in *Harold and Maude*

Jackie Gleason, comic actor, best known for his role in "The Honeymooners"

Charles Dickens, writer, author of *Great Expectations*

Ernie Kovacs, surrealist comic

Walt Kelley, cartoonist and political/philosophical commentator, creator of "Pogo"

Walt Disney, cartoon animation pioneer, creator of Mickey Mouse

Pat Oliphant, political cartoonist

Ishmael Reed, writer, author of *Mumbo Jumbo*

Robert Fosse, dancer, choreographer, film director, directed *Cabaret* and *All that Jazz*

George Bernard Shaw, playwright, author of *Man and Superman*

Philip Roth, writer, author of *Portnoy's Complaint*

John Cage, experimental musician

Andy Warhol, experimental artist and filmmaker

Paolo Soleri, radical architect

Alexandre Dumas, writer, author of *The Three Musketeers*

Yoko Ono, experimental musician and artist

Norman O. Brown, writer, author of *Love Against Death*

Jan Smuts, philosopher of holistic theory

Anais Nin, diarist and writer

Leon Trotsky, revolutionary and philosopher

Carl Jung, psychologist, studied Eastern mysticism and occultism

Eudora Welty, writer, author of *The Golden Apples*

Stuart Brand, publisher of *Whole Earth Catalogue*

Eleanor Roosevelt, wife of U. S. President F. D. Roosevelt

D. T. Suzuki, popularizer of Zen Buddhism
Gene Krupa, jazz drummer
Spike Jones, musician
Aldous Huxley, writer, author of *Island* and *The Doors of Perception*
Tom Stoppard, philosophical playwright
Billie Holiday, jazz singer
Ian Anderson, lead singer, flautist, member of Jethro Tull
Rita Hayworth, actress, played in *Gilda*
Malcolm Forbes, capitalist, publisher
Robert Goddard, rocketry pioneer
Lewis Carroll, writer, author of *Alice in Wonderland*
Charlotte Bronte, writer, author of *Jane Eyre*
Edgar Varese, avant garde musician
Oscar Wilde, poet and playwright, wrote *The Importance of Being Earnest*

Chapter Twentysix

Phase 23: The Widowed Queen

Capricorn Phase: Of the nature of Saturn
Image: From atop her lofty throne, a widowed queen watches a miller, who is hauling sacks of grain to the whirling mill wheel.

In Phase 22 the individual sought to redefine the whole of reality through free-wheeling philosophical, theological, and historical speculations. As she enters the Capricorn phases she has a strong desire to get back down to earth—to get a firm grasp of what is real and what is not. The Phase 23 individual starts her analysis, not with God or some other transcendant principle, but with herself, and the reality of her own situation. For if her world view can neither explain, nor help her master her *own* situation, what good is it?

Her first questions concern the basic frameworks in which she lives. What is her body like? her family? her society? the political system? What about nature and its laws? If, at this point, she wishes to take the leap into metaphysics, she generally favors theology, theosophy, or astrology—something with definite rules and structures, something that can be grasped and used.

The Phase 23 individual is always collecting new grist for her mill, always analyzing and re-analyzing new facts and experiences. Discarding one outworn analysis after another, she aspires to a world view that is ever clearer, more focused, and more elegant in its simplicity. The process is one of condensation, purification, and crystallization. Coal is being pressed into diamonds.

The Phase 23 individual carries forward the skills and values of an old tradition. At the same time she is a complete original, for she takes from tradition only what is relevant to her own purposes. Loyal to her family, and grateful for all the beneficial experiences they have provided her, she transfers that loyalty and commitment to society, and looks around for some way to repay her debt to the past. Like the widowed queen, she starts with old business: some valuable tradition that is in need of restructuring or regeneration. She goes at this task from various angles, trying her hand at first one method and then another. Eventually she stumbles onto a limited success. Then the real work begins.

Overcoming *inertia* can be a problem at first, but once she's gotten the wheels turning, once she has a method and a work schedule, she can develop *momentum*. Through her work, she may acquire money and status, and create things of beauty and utility. More importantly, she can develop self-discipline.

Self-discipline is the central axle of all productive activity. It is a magic mill that grinds out all that one desires, for discipline is the key to success in almost every sphere of activity. Strongly aware of the passage of time, and of her own mortality, the Phase 23 individual has little time to waste on this Earth. If she is to complete even half of what she has set out to do, she is going to have to develop self-discipline.

Negatively, the individual may become discouraged by the weighty obstacles in front of her, and abandon her task in a fit of frustration and hopelessness. Rather than accepting her situation, she resents her fate, and sinks into a surly depression, begrudging everyone else their happiness and good fortune.

Positively, she knows how to adapt her expectations and desires to the limitations of circumstance. However difficult her lot, she is able to find joy in it. Self-defined and self-confident, she delights in the extravagant expression of her personality and her talents.

The Phase 23 individual may be compared to Cassiopeia— revolving around the pole star in her uncomfortable throne. Like Cassiopeia, she must girdle in her energies, and resist the centrifugal force which pulls her away from her self-appointed duties. Once she has developed real character, however, it is as if she were sitting at the pole star, and stirring the heavens according to her will.

This tendency to pull back from life is also seen on an emotional and sexual level. Like the widowed queen, the Phase 23 individual is taking back emotional investments, and reinvesting them elsewhere—usually in her work, or in service to society. Personal grief, for instance, is transformed into pity for other people's suffering, and may take her into social or political work. But always she makes an account of the time and energy being spent, and the emotional or spiritual dividends being received. Afraid of being snared into burdensome relationships through her own sexual appetites, she will often avoid deeper commitments, until she has found someone with whom she can really make a home.

On a purely astrological level, the mill wheel in the image may be seen as the outer rim of the astrological chart. This "circle of houses" refers to the fixation or embodiment of celestial energies in an earthly framework. It refers to the particular place and time a soul has chosen to incarnate, and even the house and family into which it will be born. By "working the wheel"—by working with the inner resources of the astrological chart—the Phase 23 individual will find all that she needs to master the limitations of her original situation, and lay a firm foundation for a rich, happy, and productive life.

Phase 23 Examples

Malcolm Muggeridge, religious philosopher

Howard Pyle, Victorian illustrator

Noam Chomsky, studied the nature and evolution of languages, activist

Marc Edmund Jones, astrologer, developed the Sabian symbols, studied symbolism of the playing cards

Glenn Gould, pianist, Bach specialist

Jessica Mifford, author, wrote *The American Way of Death*

F. Donald Coggan, Archbishop of Canterbury

George Washington, revolutionary general and first U. S. President

Amy Vanderbilt, etiquette expert

John Rewald, art historian

Henri Langlois, film archivist

Henri Toulouse Lautrec, artist

Mae West, comic actress, played in *I'm No Angel*

Lotte Lenya, singer and actress, played Pirate Jenny in Brecht's *Threepenny Opera*

Henry Miller, writer, author of *Tropic of Cancer*
Antonia Fraser, historian, wrote *Mary, Queen of Scots*
Hermann Goering, Nazi, head of Luftwaffe
Benito Mussolini, fascist dictator of Italy
Joe Pyne, conservative commentator
Ray Cline, director of Bureau of Intelligence Research
Aristotle Onassis, shipping magnate
Maria Callas, opera singer
Coretta Scott King, widow of civil rights activist Martin Luther
    King, Jr.
Marian Anderson, opera singer
Bernadine Dohrn, SDS leader and head of Weathermen
Che Guevara, revolutionary martyr
Gordon Lightfoot, folk singer
Merle Haggard, country singer
Mary Travers, folk singer, member of Peter, Paul, and Mary
Paul Muni, actor, played in *The Life of Emile Zola*
James Mason, actor
Billie Jean King, tennis pro, feminist
Jimmy Breslin, commentator
Ellen Stewart, director of La Mama theater
Isadora Duncan, avant garde dancer, advocated a natural
    approach to dance
Henry Winkler, actor, youth idol, played Fonzie on TV's
    "Happy Days"
Emmett Kelly, sad clown
Sir Joshua Reynolds, portrait painter, first president of Royal
    Academy
Shelley Winters, actress
John Belushi, comedian, star of "Saturday Night Live"
Alice Cooper, rock singer

Chapter Twentyseven

Phase 24: The Magic Realm

Second Capricorn Phase: Of the nature of Venus, Chiron, Uranus, the Sun

Image: A magic tree in the central square of a medieval city, with the Sun in its branches and gold in its roots. A rabbit with a gold pocket watch appears suddenly, and runs around the tree, throwing the townspeople into a commotion.

> "...I behold this Kernel of an Apple, but leaving the Corporeity, I turn myself from the External Form, to the Internal Invisible Seed, and with the Eye of my Mind I contemplate the whole Tree, with the Root, Trunck, Bowes, Sprigs, Leaves, Flowers, and Fruit, comprised in One, and in due time manifested to have received its proper Body..."
>
> *A treatise of Oswaldus Crollius of signatures of Internal things*, trans. Richard Russell (1669)

In his childhood, the Phase 24 individual inhabits a world that is alive with magic. He actively dreams his existence—as if it were a vision in a crystal ball. Since boundaries do not yet exist between his conscious and unconscious mind, he thoughtlessly projects the archetypal inner forms of nature onto the outer world. This gives the world around him incredible depth and color, for he is able to see not only the physical forms of nature, but the astral and mental forms making up their inner ground. Thus, when he

IMAGE: PHASE 24

looks at the Sun, he doesn't just see a physical body giving off physical light and physical heat; he also sees the hidden Sun of the archetypal world, which shines with a supernatural brilliance.

As the Phase 24 child matures, his subconscious is inevitably clouded by fears, desires, and socially-imposed sexual repressions. Recognizing his own potential for evil, he throws up inner barricades between the conscious ego and the shadowy desires of the subconscious. The imaginative vision of the subconscious is partially lost, and the world becomes a shell of its former self—a dry husk of impenetrable external forms. Formerly, his soul had seemed boundless; now it is locked within the crystal of time and space.

What is left is a cystallized memory from the past, an inner landscape that still partakes of the divine harmony of the "World Soul." The remainder of life is spent in trying to give expression to this inner vision—to manifest a bit of heaven on Earth. This is the phase's Venusian impulse.

Venus mediates between the ideal and the real, the astral and the physical. It *crystallizes* a code of thought and behavior that gives concrete expression to one's spiritual ideals. It *clothes* one's ideals in suitable behavioral forms. Since we are dealing with a Capricorn phase, this code of conduct is based on social tradition. However, that tradition is modified and perfected until it has taken on the individualistic self-consistency of Venus. Unfortunately, some people of this phase try to impose their own codes onto others, displaying an authoritarian moralism that completely contradicts their own moral individualism.

The central vision of Phase 24 is expressed not so much in terms of behavior, as in some highly developed form of personal magic—a specialized skill developed to such high proficiency that it seems a form of magic. Through this skill, the individual secures himself a unique social niche, a socially acceptable outpost from which to practice his art. It is also through this skill that the public gains access to his magical inner world, penetrating the bark of his outer personality to the ideal or magical personality within.

There are many facets in the Phase 24 personality—some obvious and some hidden. Like the goat-fish of Capricorn, some of these components are demonic and animalistic. In fact, the psychological integration of these "shadowy," and often sexual, components, is the main challenge of the phase. While much of this psychological work takes place on an inner level, the Phase 24 individual may also find real people to play out the role of his shadow side, since tangible relationships make it easier for him to engage and resolve his inner conflicts. If the work is successful, his personality takes on a jewel-like self-consistency. In every situation, he is able to express the totality of his being.

The Phase 24 individual sees the material world as a magical projection of the archetypal world—an imperfect image, which through constant change, approximates the world of perfect forms. Since every individual is peripheral to the source of this projection, it is impossible for any one person to catch more than a glimpse or a fragment of the whole at any one time. The Phase 24 individual is deeply committed to his own view of reality, but he is also curious to see through other people's eyes, for underneath it all, he realizes that there is nothing absolute about reality. Reality is a working agreement.

Like all the Capricorn phases, Phase 24 has a strong social component. The impulse here is essentially anarchic, for the individual recognizes that any fundamental re-ordering of society must be preceded by a disintegration of its internal model of reality. By the sheer incongruity of his being, the Phase 24 individual mischievously undermines society's dominant world view. He stirs things up in such a way that any false or incomplete conceptualization will tend to fall apart. Most importantly, he challenges the blind *materialistic rationalism* that constitutes the worst side of modern society, introducing an element of magic that falls well outside the convenient explanatory categories of sex, power, and money.

Phase 24 Examples

Robert Morley, comic actor
Allen Funt, host of TV's "Candid Camera"
Sybil Leek, witch
Amelia Earhart, aviator, disappeared in flight
Salvador Dali, surrealist artist
Frank Herbert, science fiction writer, authored *Dune*
Piers Anthony, science fiction writer, author of *The Macroscope*
Charles Manley Hall, inventor of electric aluminum smelting
A. A. Houghton, industrialist, founded Corning Glass
Oskar Kokoschka, expressionist artist

Constantin Brancusi, sculptor
Annie Oakley, sharpshooter, folk hero
Charles Lindbergh, trans-Atlantic aviator
Harland Sanders, fried chicken franchiser
Lon Chaney Jr., actor, known for playing werewolf roles
Al Kilgore, creator of Bullwinkle cartoons
Ann Pennington, 1920s dance champ
Wolfgang Amadeus Mozart, composer, child prodigy
Ludwig Wittgenstein, philosopher of language
Wolfgang Pauli, physicist, noted for the Pauli exclusion
    principle
Andre Previn, conductor, classical and jazz pianist
Eugene McCarthy, U. S. senator, anti-war candidate for
    president
Stevie Wonder, musician
Charles Mingus, jazz bassist
Les McCann, jazz musician
Lionel Hampton, jazz vibraphone player
Marc Blitzstein, wrote musical score for *Threepenny Opera*
John Hollander, poet
Luigi Pirandello, writer, author of *Six Characters in Search of
    an Author*
Nikos Kazantzakis, writer, author of Zorba the Greek and
    Christ Recrucified (Phase 23?)
Margaret Thatcher, Prime Minister of Great Britain
Ozzie Nelson, band leader, TV star
Dick Martin, comedian, best known for his role on "Laugh-In"
Billie Burke, actress, played Glinda in *The Wizard of Oz*
Richard Chamberlain, actor, starred in *The Last Wave*
Katherine Hepburn, actress, starred in *The African Queen*
Dorothy Canfield Fisher, New England author, wrote *Seasoned
    Timber*
Michel de Nostradamus, seer
Fritz Perls, gestalt psychologist
George Du Maurier, artist, illustrator, contributor to *Punch*

Chapter Twentyeight

Phase 25: The Great Teacher

Third Capricorn Phase: Of the nature of Saturn, Pluto, and Mercury
Image: A great teacher enthroned in a heavy chair.
Expanded Image: A long shaft penetrates deep in the Earth, with a pool of water at the bottom. An ancient temple surrounds the pool, carved from the living stone. From a huge throne, the hierophant addresses a crowd in reverberating tones. Over the back of the throne is a jewel-studded coat of arms with gold and silver keys crossed at its center.

After a seemingly endless search, the basic components of the self have been gathered, and the personality internally balanced. Having finished with business at the periphery of life, the individual can now return to center, to the heart. If all has gone well in the previous phase, and the solar and lunar sides of the personality have been sufficiently purified, a great mystery takes place. The solar and lunar sides of the personality—the gold and silver of alchemy—are married or united, using Mercury as the intermediary. This process produces the "philosophical mercury" or "living water" of the alchemists. This is essentially the libido purified, the solar life force renewed and invigorated.

In simple terms, the solar force represents the "objective," visually apparent side of reality. The lunar force represents the whole inner side of that reality—the way one thinks and feels about it. Through compassionate intuition (Mercury), the Phase 25 individual unites both of these fields of awareness to compose a more solid and truthful picture of reality. She still trusts her eyes, and she still trusts her feelings and thoughts, but she allows the heart to make the final judgment.

Mercury adds soul to the solar and lunar qualities; it gives them life. Gold and silver are precious, but life is infinitely more precious. It is the foundation of all other values, and the basis of all relationships, the innermost point and the outermost bound. Reverence for life is like the wall around a pool: it keeps the water clean and freely flowing.

In Phase 25 the individual is married to the universal life force. She begins to see the whole in everything. She begins to see the interconnectedness of life, the shading of one thing into another, the play of lights and shadows. Actions have begun to take on overtones of past experience, for everything is now reflected in the pool of universal Memory. Other people often remind her of herself as she was at some other time in her life, or perhaps in another lifetime. When she listens to their words, she hears herself, connected by an echo from the past.

The suffering, chaos, and insanity of the world are now seen as an effect of our alienation from other people, and our alienation from life. The Phase 25 individual uses her knowledge to bridge misunderstandings and dissolve emotional barriers. She is able to penetrate to the heart of each situation, removing all that is strictly personal so that her words may resonate within other people's hearts as something of their own. She is able to speak for other people, for collectivities, for humanity. She renews the emotional bonds that hold society together—that make people respect each other and work for each other.

The Phase 25 individual is attuned to all that is timeless in life. She has re-established her ego within a matrix of ancient traditional wisdom, and from this source she borrows enormous conviction and solidity of character. She knows much of the universal order and the laws of life and death. She sits in judgment of the past, re-evaluating the events of her life in terms of the immortal Self. Much is cast aside. The pretenses and honors of the world now seem shadowy and insubstantial compared to the achievements of the soul.

Phase 25 is a phase of maturation. The soul is now old and the passions have ebbed. The individual has tired of the chase and the game, and returned to those emotions of the heart that are permanently sustaining. The life blood has been purified, the emotions refined and universalized. In her meditations the Phase 25 individual has come to empathize with the whole of life. Her heart has dissolved in the universal heart, yet the ego has remained, to teach others what she has learned.

As the last of the Earth phases, Phase 25 gives an acute awareness of the limited nature of our stay on Earth . The body is now seen as a temporary vehicle of the soul. Physical desire is being renounced—sometimes with great difficulty—because at this stage it is one more obstacle to the realization of Unity.

Phase 25 Examples

Hans Kung, liberal Swiss theologian
Danilo Dolci, the "Gandhi" of Sicily
Ralph Abernathy, civil rights leader
Dag Hammerskjold, former Secretary General of the United Nations
Malcolm X, Black political and religious leader
Dane Rudhyar, astrologer, composer, poet
Manly Palmer Hall, Theosophist, writer
Rabindranath Tagore, poet
Clifford Odets, playwright, author of *Waiting for Lefty*
Nathaniel Hawthorne, writer, author of *The Scarlet Letter*
Carson McCullers, writer, author of *A Member of the Wedding*
Wolfgang Kohler, gestalt psychologist
Ben Shahn, artist, social critic
Gabriela Mistral, poet
Mary Tyler Moore, actress
Martin Agronsky, political analyst
Anne Sexton, diarist and poet
Sylvia Plath, diarist and poet, wrote *The Bell Jar*
Alistair Cooke, author, host of TV's "Masterpiece Theatre"
Lionel Barrymore, actor, played in *Dinner at Eight*
Konstantin Stanislavsky, pioneer of "method acting"
Ben Barzman, film scenarist
Neil Diamond, pop singer
Peter Brook, director, noted for *Marat Sade*
Seymour Hersh, reporter, investigated My Lai massacre
Nathaniel West, author, wrote *The Day of the Locust*
Martha Mitchell, victim of Nixon's cover-up, Washington wife

Guy de Maupassant, writer
William Inge, playwright, author of *Picnic*
Betty Friedan, feminist leader, writer, author of *The Feminine Mystique*
William Jennings Bryan, political orator
Leo Politi, author of children's books
Lily Pons, opera singer
Arthur Rubinstein, classical pianist
Robert Casadesus, classical pianist
Claude Debussy, "impressionist" composer, occultist
Maurice Powicke, medievalist, scholar
Ed Sullivan, variety show host
Hugh Hefner, founder of the *Playboy* empire
David Lloyd George, British Prime Minister during World War I
Steve Allen, comedian

Chapter Twentynine

Phase 26: The Pied Piper

First Aquarius Phase: Of the nature of Uranus, Chiron, and Mercury
Image: The Pied Piper follows a zigzag course up a mountain of cracked glass. He wears a feathered hat, and carries a knapsack on his back. Ahead, an eagle takes flight; behind, a trail of followers, brought up in the rear by a goose.

The traditional wisdom concentrated in Phase 25 has one great flaw: it has no place for anything that is truly new. It is a summation, an end point. To go beyond it one must start anew. At Phase 26, the individual makes a complete break with the past. This frees him to embrace all that is new and vital, and to explore some of the exciting new possibilities that are in the air.

After the claustrophobic Capricorn phases, a completely new attitude is needed. First of all, the individual must lighten his load. The heavy, moralistic, (and depressing) philosophy of Capricorn is of little use now, for the individual has left behind the universities of life and is now out on the street. He needs a philosophy that is practical and immediately serviceable, a philosophy of change and passage, rather than ultimate ends. Nothing is predictable anymore; he must be willing to go forward on a simple faith in his own spiritual instincts, and follow the "white feather of Truth" wherever it may lead. The journey will be easier if he travels light; all he really needs is optimism, high spirits, a sense of opportunity...and maybe a change of underwear.

IMAGE: PHASE 26

The Phase 26 individual is usually really different—in his attitudes, behavior, appearance, sometimes even his body. Since it is somewhat difficult for him to fit in, he generally finds himself somewhere on the fringes of human society. With this change of viewpoint, he starts to see the contradictions of society with shattering clarity. Society now appears completely arbitrary and out of step with nature, a fortress with a mass of frightened people huddling behind it. As a firm believer in humanity's capacity for evolution, the Phase 26 individual holds a different vision of society: a utopian vision where freedom, equality, individuality, and the pursuit of truth play a central role. While he doesn't know exactly how to step into this vision, he knows that the first step is to prepare himself for the change, to become a citizen of the new order.

To succeed in his quest, the Phase 26 individual must not allow himself to become acculturated, so he removes himself to society's outer limits, where he can remain untamed, unbroken, and careless of society's judgments. Refusing to accept the maze-like compartmentalization of society, he makes a point of familiarizing himself with many different kinds of people and many different cultures. He becomes an expert at getting around social barriers, and failing at that, he breaks right through them.

Having rejected society's established patterns of behavior, the Phase 26 individual has to think for himself. He has to respond quickly and creatively to every situation, for his life has become an endless string of changes. Any kind of inflexibility—whether it is bred of fear, desire, duty, or circumstance—is potentially crippling, since it could lead him to miss his best opportunities. Physical mobility is especially important. If possibilities for growth dry up in one place, he has to be ready to pick up and move where the "action" is.

To remain open and unprejudiced in his approach to life, the Phase 26 individual rids himself of much of his mental baggage. He holds on to very little from the past—just a few key memories that sum up or crystallize his experience. Since his situation is too novel to be able to fall back on experience, he puts his trust in direct perception. Through practice, he develops the power of instantaneous analysis. He learns to view each situation coldly and objectively, as if through a jewel, abstracting its main elements to form a crude working model. Such models are not meant to be universally applicable, merely serviceable; they provide an immediate basis for action.

If the Phase 26 individual loses track of his ideals, his life quickly loses all direction. He may then degenerate into an irresponsible drifter, a derelict, or a criminal. Incapable or unwilling to learn from his mistakes, he gets caught up in one unpleasant imbroglio after another. Since he never loses his wild Uranian energy, he will still manage to magically attract peculiar situations and events, except now those situations will tend to be hassles rather than opportunities.

The Phase 26 individual is motivated by the will to wholeness. Thus, while he is open to all experiences, all ideas, and all people, he is especially drawn to those situations that will strengthen his weaknesses, and add to his independence. He would eventually like to become completely self-sufficient, resting, like the Sun, entirely above the limitations of earthly existence.

Phase 26 Examples

Henry David Thoreau, naturalist, writer, author of *Walden Pond*

Joseph Smith, Mormon leader

Lord Baden Powell, founder of the Boy Scouts

Marcus Garvey, Black leader, led "back to Africa" movement

Ivan Illich, advocated abolishing schools

Robert Heinlein, science fiction writer, author of *Stranger in a Strange Land*

Gurdjeiff, spiritual seeker, teacher, adventurer

Alexander Dubcek, liberalized Czechoslovakia, crushed by Russians

Salvador Allende, Marxist Chilean leader, overthrown by CIA-led coup

Ted Turner, independent network TV executive, sportsman

Joe Namath, football quarterback

Frank Sinatra, singer and pop idol

Bette Midler, comedienne, actress, starred in *Ruthless People*

Gale Storm, singer, actress, TV's "My Little Margie"

Tony Richardson, film director, made *Tom Jones*

Sam Peckinpah, film director, known for depictions of violence in films

Bonnie Parker, outlaw

Ian Fleming, author of the James Bond books

Robert Newton, actor, played Long John Silver in *Treasure Island*

Gillo Pontecorvo, director, directed *Battle of Algiers*
Sergei Eisenstein, film director, made *Alexander Nevsky*
Vance Packard, consumer advocate
Phyllis Diller, offbeat comedienne
John Gardner, politician, head of Common Cause
Betty Furness, consumer advisor
Agnolo di Cosimo, Renaissance "mannerist" noted for developing a distortion of the human form
E. F. Kripling, entomologist, worked with screw worm sterilization program
Saul Bellow, writer, author of *Mr. Sandler's Planet* and *Herzog*
Maurice Bejart, choreographer
Roman Polanski, filmmaker, made *Rosemary's Baby* and *Repulsion*
Howard Hughes, eccentric millionaire
Patrick McGoohan, actor in TV's "The Prisoner"
Roy C. Andrews, explorer
Sir Henry Shackleton, Antarctic explorer
Wasily Kandinsky, abstract expressionist artist
Piet Mondrian, abstract artist
Franz Marc, abstract artist
Henri Matisse, fauve artist
Ernst Kirchner, abstract expressionist artist
Alberto Giacometti, abstract sculptor
Grock, famous clown
Elmer Sperry, inventor of the gyroscope

Chapter Thirty

Phase 27: The Saint

Second Aquarius Phase: Of the nature of Pallas, Venus, Neptune, and Mercury
Image: A beautiful woman is seated by a spring surrounded by forget-me-nots. At her side is a large open book. A heron stands in front of her on one leg and contemplates the large egg in its nest.

In Phase 26, the individual moved restlessly through the world collecting anything that might heighten her physical and spiritual independence. Entering Phase 27, she slowly awakens to the fact that she will find real happiness and contentment only within herself. So she ceases her wandering, settles down in a pleasant spot, and nurtures her blossoming new awareness in quiet contemplation.
   This is the most mystical of the phases. It marks a reabsorbtion into the harmony of nature, a return to that state of original grace beyond the polarity of life and death. People of this phase expect little from the world, at least as far as their desires go. Most of their concentration is directed inwards, towards a peaceful inner vision that partakes of both dream and fantasy. In their meditations, Phase 27 individuals recollect all of their most expansive and illumined moments, distilling and purifying the timeless spiritual light which animates these memories. Specifics of time and place are forgotten as they supend themselves within a field of living light. The ego melts away in self-forgetfulness, and

the soul is freed from its fear of death. The individual is finally free to breathe, to expand and explore. She has recaptured the sweet serenity of childhood, and sits like a child, enveloped in the light of an endless summer day.

By Phase 27, the individual's life energy has ceased to flow out towards the world. Now it is flowing inwards and downwards. Through memory she travels back to the source of her consciousness, back beyond her birth to that shining empty space of undifferentiated life energy from which all things come. She travels back to the Cosmic Egg, where the original idea for the world is still in one piece.

Life on Earth is a whole, but we are separated from that whole when we are born and begin to individuate. From that moment we start to forget all the thoughts and feelings of the whole, and begin to think exclusively in terms of our own personal needs and wishes. Our memories of other species have begun to revolve around their usefulness or harmfulness to us.

By contrast, the young child is still at peace with the world. It can feel the moods of the world as easily as it relates to its everyday needs. This childlike attunement is what the Phase 27 individual is trying to recapture. But unlike the child, she has already gone through the cycle of individuation, and has realized what a tiny part of the whole she really is. With this shrinking sense of self-importance, she has become better able to see the divine in other things. Every point has become a sun, pouring forth the living light. What is not God is now seen to be an illusion, an incorrect way of seeing things and thinking about things which posits the self as the center of the Universe, when the self is only a mirror of the center—no less a center than anything else, but also no more. The Phase 27 individual is aware that the manifest world is only a fractured image of the truth, and will always be marred by the illusions of ego and separateness, fear and desire. And while this knowledge holds great sadness for her, it is a sadness that is washed away in an overflowing love for life.

The Phase 27 individual is calm and detached in her passage through the world, but she is also very much a participant. Having no individual center to protect, she is open to other people, easily empathizing with different points of view. Her influence on others is subtle and permeating. She unwittingly acts as a catalyst, planting seeds of higher consciousness in all who meet her. Since she speaks from the heart, from the center of all things, her words have a strangely far-reaching effect, striking a sympathetic chord even in those who would seem unreceptive. The alchemists called this type of consciousness the *Great Elixir* or *Great Medicine*, since it acts from within to make all things whole.

In Phase 27 the individual tries to recover her sense of belonging in the Universe. In less evolved individuals this spiritual quest is replaced by a more or less primitive desire to return to the mother's breast. Meditation is replaced by comforting fantasies, and the heart is wrapped in glamorous dreams of refined sensuality. These people still feel much generosity and love towards others, but this is tainted by a subtle spiritual evasiveness, for they have made no real commitment to the inner light. Rather than righting themselves, these individuals continue to play by the edge of the karmic whirlpool. They are still in the cycle, moving the world and being moved by it.

To succeed here, the individual can be neither too inward nor too outward. If she is too inward, she will become self-absorbed, and start relating to the world as if it were a daydream. If she is too outward, she will dissipate her inner light in perceptions and desires. Consciousness must find the exact balance point. Just as a mason uses a plumb line to lay the foundation of a building, the Phase 27 individual must exercise a keen sense of inner balance, in order to lay the foundation for an immortal spiritual consciousness.

Phase 27 Examples

A. A. Milne, children's book writer, author of *Winnie the Pooh*
Norman Rockwell, illustrator
Dante Gabriel Rosetti, Pre-Raphaelite painter, poet
Stephen Foster, songwriter, wrote "Beautiful Dreamer" and "Old Kentucky Home"
Fred Rogers, TV's "Mister Rogers"
Bob Keeshan, TV's "Captain Kangaroo"
Gertrude Berg, actress, starred in "I Remember Mama"
Victor Herbert, composer, wrote *Babes in Toyland*
Edgar Rice Burroughs, author of the Tarzan series
Ira Progoff, psychologist with a spiritual orientation
Ferde Grofe, composer, wrote *Grand Canyon Suite*
J. D. Salinger, writer, best known for *Catcher in the Rye*
William Faulkner, writer, author of *As I Lay Dying* and *The Sound and the Fury*

John Gielgud, Shakespearean actor
Rudolf Serkin, classical pianist (Phase 28?)
Marc Chagall, artist, known for creating dream-like images
Maurits Escher, surrealist artist
Jean Arp, sculptor
Jean Louis, coutourier, designed "body stocking"
Angela Lansbury, actress, star of TV's "Murder She Wrote"
Sebastian Cabot, actor on TV's "Checkmate"
Stan Laurel, comic actor
St. Frances Cabrini, religious worker
Father Damien, priest who worked in a leper colony
Cesar Chavez, labor leader
Russell Oberlin, counter tenor
Carla Fracci, opera singer
Arthur Rimbaud, symbolist poet
Carlo Levi, author, wrote *Christ Stopped at Eboli*
Deborah Kerr, actress, played in *The King and I*
Tony Perkins, actor, star of *Psycho*
Paul Stookey, folk singer, member of Peter, Paul, and Mary
Herbert Hoover, U. S. President at the time of the Stock
   Market Crash that led to Depression
Calvin Coolidge, U. S. President, nicknamed "Silent Cal"
Robert Millikan, physicist, did experiments with light
Frank Lloyd Wright, modern architect
Derek Jacobi, actor, played lead role in *I, Claudius*
Henry Nusselein, spiritualist
Elisabeth Kubler-Ross, writer, author of *On Death and Dying*
Immanuel Kant, philosopher, author of *Critique of Pure
   Reason*

Chapter Thirtyone

Phase 28: The Prophet

Third Aquarius Phase: Of the nature of Pluto and Saturn
Image: A bearded man dressed in filthy animal skins approaches a farming community situated at the confluence of two river valleys. Looking into the Sun, he makes out haystacks and buildings. Coming closer, he sees a man reaping with a scythe, while others winnow, plow and sow.

From his vantage point at the end of the cycle, the Phase 28 individual is afforded an awe-inspiring vista of his entire past, and even a few flashes from the future. What was once a confusing collage of unrelated experiences, images, and impressions has taken on a distinct shape. He is like a passenger on a train that has just turned a sharp corner, opening up a sweeping view of the entire mountain range he had been passing through when the train turns a sharp corner. The broad outlines of his destiny are now clear— where he has come from and where he is going.

The Phase 28 individual is no longer able to separate himself from the life around him. He is witness to an old order dying and a new order being born. These changes will affect everyone equally; *personal* goals are being eclipsed by the needs of the situation.

Life is a single organism, an intricate web of karmic connections that is constantly evolving towards greater consciousness and greater freedom. When people acknowledge life's interdependence, and work together to solve their mutual problems, then their communities grow and prosper. But when human institutions are allowed to calcify, decay and death are just down the road. There is no tragedy in this. Death is absolutely necessary to the life process. It is the drive gear of change, sweeping away the old to make room for the new. What is most fit survives and multiplies, and over long periods of time the face of the planet changes and evolves, molting its outer forms like a snake shedding its skin.

The Phase 28 individual sees the changing physical surface of life as reality's outermost skin—a mere end-product of countless internal processes. Placing little value on external appearances, he looks through them with the glazed stare of a passenger at the window of a train. His focus reaches deeper—to the invisible laws of manifestation and change that form the underpinnings of reality.

In the symbol we see farmers reaping and sowing. Through an understanding of natural processes, and especially natural cycles, the farmer manipulates nature to his own benefit. Similarly, the Phase 28 individual studies the cycles of history, economics, astrology, or evolution in order to determine if, when, and how he should *act*. At times there is little to be done, for the karmic net behind his situation is rigid and inflexible. In such situations, he may simply take his place among the other players and passively duplicate some internal script, as it rolls out into the future. At other times the situation is more fluid, due to a momentary balance of power. He then tries to predict where the major lines of force are going to cross, and rushes out to meet the crisis, armed with whatever social power he can muster: money, political clout, or power of persuasion. If drastic personal measures are required, he will use them. However, such individual actions are rarely adequate to the situation. He therefore tries to mobilize the community, advising them of the crisis in such clear terms that their choice would seem inevitable. It is this clarity of vision, this ability to sum up a situation in some unforgettable image, that makes the Phase 28 individual such a seminal force in the activation of new social and cultural impulses.

On a personal level, the Phase 28 individual is just as much the catalyst. He is like the *mysterious stranger* thrown inexplicably across one's path at some significant juncture of life. Looking only to the bare bones of the situation, he refuses to acknowledge other people's mythologies and rationalizations. By allowing reality to act through him, he awakens others to the limitations of their consciousness, in a kind of psychic T'ai Chi.

He himself may attract people of the same ilk— personifications of his own subconscious complexes, in search of release. By recognizing his karmic connections to these people, and relating to them with clarity and detachment, he is able to rid himself of reality-distorting personality fragments. The images of the soul or "passionate body" are thus unwound like the bandages of a mummy, and the soul is reborn into a life of pure spirit.

At Phase 28 the personal ego is disintegrating. Desires, selfish motives, petty ambitions, and subconscious complexes are being sloughed off, as the individual moves to his predestined spot within the historical drama. Negatively, he is unable to let go. Overwhelmed by a fear of death, he surrounds himself with symbols of personal importance: money, power, and prestige. But he has no existential ground, and when death comes, he is unprepared. Unwilling to give freely to life, his relationships take on the character of business transactions. Convinced that he is being cheated by his enemies, or by his own evil fate, he lashes out at life with destructive fury.

At the end of the waning hemicycle, consciousness is becoming impersonal, disembodied, and universal. There is a colorlessness to thought that makes it easy for others to adopt and personalize. *Intellectual* consciousness is thus passing into the genius of the race. After physical death it will *haunt* the race—as an angelic consciousness, if the individual was highly evolved, or a demonic consciousness, if he had allowed himself to degenerate. Meanwhile the *soul*, having shed the physical, astral, and *intellectual* bodies, is free to pass into the Heavenly Vision of Phase 1, to find union with the Light, or to swirl quickly around it, and be flung once more into the Cycle of Incarnation.

Phase 28 Examples

Havelock Ellis, pioneer in sexual research, symbolic alchemist
Konstantin Tsiolkovsky, early prophet of space flight
Karl Marx, communist theoretician
Georgia O'Keeffe, pioneering painter (Phase 1?)
Niels Bohr, nuclear physicist, known for the Manhattan Project
John Maynard Keynes, economist, proponent of deficit spending

Philo T. Farnsworth, television inventor
Rod Serling, host and writer for "The Twlight Zone"
Richard Avedon, photographer
Richard Boone, actor, star of TV's "Have Gun Will Travel"
Leroi Jones (Imamu Amiri Baraku), Black militant,
  playwright
Herblock, political cartoonist
Jack Anderson, journalist
Barbara Jordan, politician, professor
Studs Terkel, journalist, writer, author of *Working*
Brian Aldiss, science fiction writer, author of *Cryptozoic*
C. Wright Mills, sociologist, wrote *The Power Elite*
David Rockefeller, banker, founder of Trilateral Commission
Cecil Rhodes, colonialist, Prime Minister of the Cape Colony,
  developed "Rhodesia" (now Zimbabwe)
Baron Rothschild, financier
Arthur Schlesinger Jr., liberal historian
Heinrich Muller, head of German Gestapo
Meir Kahane, leader of Jewish Defense League
Vyacheslav Chornovil, Soviet dissident
Jane Jacobs, progressive urban reformer
Desiderius Erasmus, Dutch theologian and Renaissance
  scholar
Florence LaRue, Black feminist lawyer
John Dos Passos, writer, author of *Manhattan Transfer* and
  Orient Express
Norbert Wiener, computer technologist
Ludwig van Beethoven, classical composer
Marlon Brando, actor, starred in *The Wild One* and *On the
  Waterfront*
Colette, writer, author of *Gigi*
Algernon Swinburne, pre-Raphaelite poet
George Wallace, Governor of Alabama, resisted desegregation
Federico Fellini, filmmaker, known for *Juliet of the Spirits, 8
  1/2,* and *Amarcord*
Henry Cabot Lodge Jr., Lyndon Johnson's ambassador to
  Vietnam
Gino Severini, futurist artist
Bill Mauldin, political cartoonist, famous for "The Bomb"
John Barth, author, wrote *The Sot Weed Factor*
Otis Chandler, ruthless publishing magnate

Chapter Thirtytwo

The System

While the division of the lunar cycle into twenty-eight phases is fairly straightforward, the Moon phases have an underlying structure that is extremely complex, involving interpenetrating cones and mutually dependent "faculties" of the soul. It is hard to say whether Yeats himself understood this system. Since his book was based on channeled information, it's quite possible that he didn't. In any case, he didn't do a very good job explaining it.

After years of study, and some helpful explanations from astrologer Rick Klimczak, I finally figured out the system. And once I understood it, I realized that it wasn't that difficult. The real problem was in the organization of the ideas rather than in the ideas themselves, for Yeats had made the mistake of introducing his most difficult concepts at the beginning of the book, before the reader had any idea what the system as a whole was about. Rather than repeating Yeats' mistake, let's put aside the faculties for the time being, and start by examining some of the more basic concepts.

The lunar cycle may be aptly compared to the growth cycle of a plant. The new Moon may be compared to the germination of the seed, the early waxing phases to the growth of the plant, and the late waxing phases to the onset of flowering. The full Moon may be likened to the ripening of the fruit, the early waning phases to the decay of the fruit, and the late waning phases to the formation of the seed. And then the cycle starts over. The vegetative symbolism is appropriate because of its absolute regularity. One generation follows another with only the smallest variation.

Things are not as clear when we start applying the system to people. Employing the same sort of analogy, we could say that the new Moon represents infancy, the waxing phases represent childhood and early adulthood, and the full Moon represents courtship and reproduction. But what then? If our sole purpose as human beings were the perpetuation of the species, then what is the use of the waning half of the cycle? If it were merely a preparation for death, then why are individuals of later phases so attentive to their inner development? Can it be that the cycle simply ends at Phase 28, that after all our painstaking transformations, we are suddenly whisked off into heaven or hell? The fact is, it is impossible to understand the lunar cycle without bringing in the theory of reincarnation.

The lunar cycle represents a complex dialectic between spirit and form—which are philosophy's simplified terms for the *solar principle* and the *lunar principle*. At the new Moon, the solar principle is dominant, for the world is conceived in terms of spiritual essences. At the full Moon, the lunar principle is dominant, for the world is seen in terms of concrete forms. The entire cycle can be viewed as a movement of spirit into matter, and its subsequent disengagement and return to the world of the Mind. The philosophy that is implied is essentially Eastern. The soul incarnates in order to gain worldly experience (the waxing phases). Then, through meditation and reflection, it transforms this experience into spiritual wisdom (the waning phases). Since this wisdom is deathless it follows the soul around the wheel into its next incarnation. After many lifetimes, the soul finally succeeds in freeing itself from the wheel of karma and the passionate struggle of opposites.

While certain elements of this philosophy may suffer from cultural distortion, it is in basic harmony with the Moon phases and most other occult systems. It is little wonder, then, that occultists have been so eager to embrace the doctrine of reincarnation. It explains rather than confuses; it makes sense.

Note that orthodox Christianity rejects occultism's cyclic cosmology for a linear and dualistic view of the cosmos. Furthermore, what it does borrow from the lunar mysteries is highly distorted. In Christian theology Phase 1 has become the Kingdom of Heaven—blissful, ethereal, perfect, and bodiless. Phase 15 has become The World—realm of sin, temptation, and degradation. This is a total misrepresentation, a priestly device to crucify humankind between the unreal concepts of pure spirit and pure matter. It is also a deviation from true Christian doctrine—a Manichaean idea grafted onto Christianity by St. Augustine, for the basest of political motives.

Early Christians believed that Christ would bring the Kingdom to Earth, by overthrowing and destroying earthly tyrannies. This belief gave rise to millenial expectations and radical political movements. If the Kingdom of God could manifest on Earth, it was clear that the Earth had divine potential; there was no real reason to put up with poverty and oppression.

As long as Christianity was a minority religion, this form of social agitation was more or less accepted. However, when the Church became the state religion of Rome, these hopes for the earthly Kingdom became an embarrassment. Acting as an agent of Rome, St. Augustine, in his *City of God*, removed the Kingdom from Earth to heaven. Christ's Kingdom would never come to the Earth, for the Earth was the realm of Satan. There was nothing of value, nor could there be anything of value on Earth. The true Christian, therefore, should accept the trials of earthly existence as a punishment for the Fall, and place all hope in the Kingdom of Heaven.

This piece of theological trickery had terrible consequences for Western civilization.

•In the lunar cosmology, Phases 1 and 15 are not opposites; they are polarities—polarities that form part of a unified and ongoing cycle. To view them as opposites is to set spirit against form, sky against Earth, humanity against nature, and ultimately, man against woman. •

The cyclical view of the cosmos is in harmony with nature and all its processes. It describes a world of growth, decay, and regeneration. It describes a world of gradual evolution. It does not threaten the individual with an illusory choice between salvation and damnation. Such dualistic concepts are products of the mind, and have no place in nature.

To further explore the difference between the cyclical and dualistic points of view, let's take a closer look at Phases 1 and 15.

Phase 1

Phase 1 represents the spiritual overmind, the ideal world as it exists in the mind of God. Though it is complete in itself, it is imbalanced in that image and essence have as yet no *intrinsic* connection to matter and form. Since the Sun and Moon are conjunct at the new Moon, Phase 1 has no sense of perspective; consciousness is inspired and visionary, but may also lapse into presumptuous egocentricity and infantile unconsciousness. In the highly evolved individual, Phase 1 may represent a blissful immersion in God-consciousness, but for the immature soul it can signify a helplessly dependent and childish outlook on the world. It's all a matter of which coil of the spiral you are on.

Phase 1 is the spiritual reality on which the Christian conception of heaven was based. For most people this is not a valid spiritual goal, for it represents a longing to return to a state of infancy, where one was surrounded by love, and all of one's needs were being met by others. But infancy cannot be reclaimed. We inevitably lose our innocence as we grow older. And that is as it should be, because if we are going to learn anything from life, we are going to have to get into life; we are going to have to get our hands dirty.

One of the chief mysteries of the Moon is its ability to recover its innocence, its virginity. This is not accomplished by shrinking from life. It is natural for us to immerse ourselves in sensory experience during the youthful phases of our souls' development. Yet it is equally natural for the older soul to discard those elements of experience which it has outgrown. Thus, in the waning phases individual consciousness is steadily withdrawn from the external world—a process which eventually returns the individual to a state of spiritual simplicity, which is as much wisdom as it is innocence.

Phase 15

Phase 15 represents the material world as a perfectly realized balance of physical and spiritual laws. Just as the Moon's light is a reflection of the Sun's light, the material forms of Phase 15 are essentially reflections of the spiritual forms found in Phase 1. Matter may have its own existence, but its meaning and coherence are ultimately derived from the world of the spirit. Thus, while Phase 15 is the most incarnated of the phases, it is nonetheless penetrated by spirit, which serves as it organizing principle.

Phase 15 is ruled by Virgo, the sign of the harvest. Virgo gives a strong sense of the beauty, fertility, and goodness of the Earth. Here we see Nature and all her beautiful forms as a materialized expression of God and God's love for the Earth. While orthodox and gnostic Christians have styled the Earth as a place of ugliness and misery, the Virgoan vision of Phase 15 sees in the beauty of Nature a self-evident testimony of God's love for the Earth, and the possibility of a fruitful and harmonious cooperation between Heaven and Earth.

To understand Phases 1 and 15 one must understand the difference between an occult polarity and a philosophical contrary. In an occult polarity similar issues are approached from opposing points of view. There may be conflicts, but these conflicts can be bridged through honest communication, and forged into a new and higher level of consciousness. This same type of relationship is found in oppositions between Moon phases, zodiacal signs, and planets.

The aspect of the opposition, for instance, is essentially an aspect of consciousness expansion. The aspect is associated with occasional periods of tension and discomfort, but these feelings tend to dissolve with the dawning of a more inclusive perspective. Unlike the square, which demands action, the opposition functions largely within the mind. It may, at times, get stuck in some internal "holy war," but this is a problem of its own making, and is usually resolved through a simple change of attitude.

The polarities of occult philosophy are certainly less precise than the pleasingly simple dualisms of philosophy and religion. They are also less violent. Most of humanity's violence is rooted in dualistic philosophy and religion. Occult philosophy, by contrast, brings with it the ways of peace, for it is in tune with Nature and Nature's path—the path of gradual evolution.

Waxing and Waning Phases

Phases 1 and 15 divide the lunar cycle into two halves: the waxing and waning hemicycles (see Figure 32.1). This is the clearest and most important division of the lunar cycle, differentiating two very different types of human psychology.

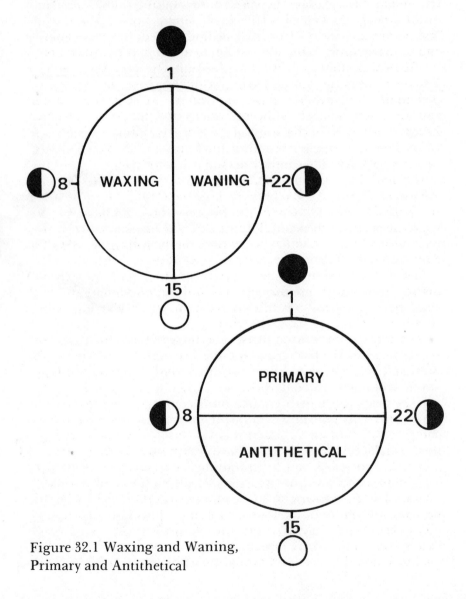

Figure 32.1 Waxing and Waning,
Primary and Antithetical

Since Phase 1 represents the spiritual overmind and Phase 15 represents the manifest creation, the early phases—the phases of the waxing Moon—represent a progressive incarnation of spirit into matter. These are the phases of youth. They are concerned with mastery—mastery of personal faculties, and mastery of the world. Just as a child must learn to actualize its innate powers of speech, movement, thought, and expression, the waxing phase individual must bring spiritual gifts into some kind of concrete manifestation. This person is constantly discovering, developing and strengthening skills, and testing them out in the environment.

Because of their association with youth, the waxing phases give a sense of personal importance, personal power, and unlimited potentiality. Desires are simple and for the most part attainable, and life is approached with enthusiasm and innocent optimism. People born during the waxing phases are riding with the life force. They don't have to give too much thought to their direction; they can just trust their instincts and push forward.

At best, these people are bringing light, energy, and power into the world. They are embodying their own spiritual visions in their personalities, and then trying to impress these visions onto the world at large. Innocent and optimistic, they fully expect to find their ideals of love and beauty within the world itself, and when they can not find them, they simply create them.

Negatively, the waxing phases represent the "fall" of spirit into matter. Spiritual energy may be constantly down-graded, and with it consciousness, until it has arrived at a jaded sexuality and a cynical and shortsighted materialism.

Notice that the waxing phases are framed by two fire signs—the Aries phases at the beginning and the Leo phases at the end. The waxing hemicycle has a lot of fire; it is vital, creative, visionary, adventurous, and strong-willed.

The waning phases are much more complex. From the cosmic perspective, people of the later phases have already spiritually completed the early goals of life. Thus they really only come into their own later in life, after they have grown up, had their fun, and established their families. The waning phases are coming to grips with an inevitable decline in physical energy. This brings up many issues, including aging, death, and the meaning of life. With a growing awareness of their own mortality, people of the waning phases begin to withdraw from the physical world and re-center themselves within their minds. Worldly experience is absorbed, analyzed, and digested, and brought back to the mental level. By the time they have arrived at Phase 22, they have developed a sense of abstraction from life—a sense of being in the world but not of it.

In the waning phases existential questions are acute. People can no longer justify themselves in terms of their personal lives; they are too aware of life's transcience. They seek a form of immortality by identifying themselves with philosophical and religious ideals that will live on beyond them. They take their place within some larger historical movement, and dedicate their lives to a vision of social and spiritual revitalization.

Individuals of the waning phases have extremely complex minds. They are constantly rethinking their experiences, and extracting from them a more penetrating and comprehensive understanding of the world. During the waxing phases, the spirit was being embodied in matter. During the waning phases, personas and world views are being shed like the skins of a snake, as these people gradually withdraw their energies from the world—retracting their projections in order to reclaim their autonomy, and their spiritual and psychological freedom.

Positively, waning phase individuals are effective catalysts in the evolution of human consciousness. Negatively, their mental complexities lead them into empty byways. They lose their energy and enthusiasm, and fall in to all kinds of ruts. Unwilling or unable to rid themselves of accumulated emotional and intellectual baggage, they slowly slip into the rigidity, stuffiness, and defeatism so often associated with older people.

Notice that the waning phases are framed by two air signs: Libra and Aquarius. This helps to explain the intellectual and philosophical interests commonly cultivated by waning phase individuals, as well as their search for truth, and their desire to participate in the intellectual and cultural life of society.

Solar and Lunar Streams

The waxing and waning phases of the Moon are driven by two completely different types of energy. The waxing phases may be called solar in that they are energetic, outgoing, straightforward, and strongly self-aware. The waning phases may be called lunar in that they are pensive, complex, reflective, and concerned with society and the environment.

Even better terms for the two halves of the cycle can be found outside the field of astrology. The two active elements in alchemy are called Sulfur and Mercury. Sulfur is the element associated with the waxing phases. It is the active, incarnating element, and is related to will and desire. Mercury is the element associated with the waning phases. It is the transformative element, and is related to the soul and the spiritual intelligence. The relationship of Sulfur and Mercury to the Moon phases is symbolized clearly in the Wheel of Fortune card of Paul Foster Case's tarot.

Figure 32.2 The Wheel of Fortune (Paul Foster Case's Tarot)

The serpent crawling down the left side of the wheel represents "cosmic radiant energy"[1] as it descends into "name and form."[2] The snake is obviously another symbol for the "sulfurous" or "solar" stream which energizes the waxing phases.

On the right side of the the wheel we see the jackal-headed figure of Hermanubis, an Egyptian version of Hermes or Mercury. Since Anubis is a god of the underworld, Hermanubis refers specifically to Mercury's role in guiding souls to and from the underworld, which symbolically speaking, is simply the world of matter and form, as represented by Phase 15.

Hermanubis refers to the Mercurial Principle that animates the waning phases, and especially to the process of decomposition by which the soul is liberated from the domination of the body. Note the alchemical symbols for Sulfur and Mercury in the illustration,

Figure 32.3 ⚹ and ☿

which unfortunately have not been placed alongside the appropriate hemicycles.

Ida and Pingala

In Indian occultism one finds a variant of the solar and lunar streams in the Pingala and the Ida. These are two energy pathways in the etheric body, generally represented as two serpents coiled around the spinal cord.

Pingala, or "solar breath," is hot and fiery; it is the energy which descends from the higher etheric centers of the body and is used in all external, desire-related activities.

Ida, or "lunar breath," is cold and moist. It is associated with catabolic physical processes, the involuntary muscles of the body, and dream and trance states. Since Ida leads from the lower seats of consciousness to the higher ones, it is also associated with spiritual evolution.

Since the Ida and Pingala fit in so perfectly with two important elements of the Moon phases, one may wonder whether other elements of Indian occultism—chakras, for instance—also have their equivalents in the Moon phases. But more on that later.

The Four Faculties

The innermost cog in Yeats' astrological system is made up of four quasi-psychological "faculties," known as Will, Mask, Creative Mind, and Body of Fate. Since the faculties have no counterpart in traditional astrology, they can easily become a stumbling block to understanding Yeats' system, especially since they are never clearly explained. The following passage is the closest thing to a systematic definition. It is a bit difficult, and bears rereading:

"The *Four Faculties* are not the abstract categories of philosophy, being the result of the four memories of the Daimon or ultimate self of that man. His *Body of Fate,* the series of events forced upon him from without, is shaped out of the *Daimon's* memory of the events of his past incarnations; his *Mask* or object of desire or idea of the good, out of its memory of the moments of exaltation in his past lives; his *Will* or normal ego out of its memory of all the events of his present life, whether consciously remembered or not; his *Creative Mind* from its memory of ideas— or universals—displayed by actual men in past lives, or their spirits between lives."[3]

Well, that gives us something to work with, but it is also pretty vague. Fortunately, we can infer a lot about the faculties from the rest of the system. Yeats gives us the real clue when he informs us that "...*Will* predominates during the first quarter, *Mask* during the second, *Creative Mind* during the third, *Body of Fate* during the fourth."[4] Once you have gotten a feel for the four quarters, this clarifies things considerably, since the effects of the faculties within their own zones of influence are pretty obvious.

The Will

Looking closely at the phases of the first quarter, it is clear that the faculty of Will is very straightforward. Not unlike the common conception, it implies the will to live, and the will to prevail in worldly activities.

The faculty of Will becomes operative at the new Moon, which is symbolically related to conception and physical birth. The phases immediately following the new Moon are phases of childhood—and children, as everyone knows, have very strong wills. The first phase of the quarter—the keynote phase—is associated with the sign Pisces. This may seem a little strange, since Pisces isn't considered a particularly willful sign. However, in Pisces we find the same sense of divine attunement that we find in children, the same sense of being loved by the Universe, that gives a child its radiant self-confidence.

The young child has not yet differentiated its own will from the divine will. Children have an innate trust in their own motivations, and are therefore direct, forceful, and unself-conscious in exercising their wills.

The early Moon phases are related, among other things, to the development of motor skills. Through a combination of instinct and experience, the child is learning how to give his or her body the right mental commands in the right order. Children use a similar approach with the outside world, for they assume that the world, like their bodies, will give them what they want if it is only approached in the right way. Life isn't needlessly complicated, and when a problem does arise, they look for quick and practical solutions.

The Will gives a courageous and optimistic outlook on life, and a self-reliant attitude in dealing with problems. Its main drawback is that it assumes a kind of omnipotence ("Where there's a will, there's a way."). This may result in a childishly oversimplified view of the world.

The Will is action-oriented and centered in the present. According to Yeats, it is based on memories from the present life. It can be more accurately described as a sharp sense of self-awareness, focused within the present, and actively attuned to all the real possibilities of one's situation.

The Mask

The Mask is at its strongest in the second quarter, which extends from Phase 8 to Phase 15. The Mask is much more complex than the Will. However, an understanding of Phase 8 gives us most of what we need to know, since it is at this point that the individual stops conforming to inherited social roles and starts to develop an individualistic social persona.

Phase 8 is a Gemini phase, involved in personality development and the differentiation of the Mask from the Shadow,

• At Phase 8 people's best traits are being separated from their worst traits, their highest hopes from their worst fears. The birth of the Mask represents an entrance into the world of illusion, for it is here that people start running away from their Shadows, and running towards their dreams. It is here that desire is born. ✔

Unlike the Will, which is related to the central Self, the Mask is never fully embodied, but seems to occupy a timeless realm that is only approximated in any real life situation. People can certainly try to live within the images of the Mask, but in a way this is always an act, which derives as much of its reality from other people's reactions as it does from any intrinsic substance.

The Mask is born in a Gemini phase, and like Gemini it is slippery and evasive. Developmentally, it is related to adolescence. The innocence of childhood is being lost, as the individual runs up against society and all of its frustrating and artificial standards. A certain phoniness may intrude into the personality, as the individual tries to imitate current styles of social and sexual attractiveness. Socially unacceptable emotions are hidden or redirected, and this may result in a splitting of the personality into the conflicting elements of Mask and Shadow.

As the lunar cycle progresses from Phase 8 to Phase 15, from the forward square to the full Moon, one is leaving behind the world of the spirit and entering into the world of matter. The Mask presides over this transition and is responsible for the translation of spiritual forms into material forms. The social compromises of adolescence, and of the Gemini Moon phase, can therefore be seen as part of the more general problem of translating spiritual ideals into viable worldly forms. This process always involves compromise, for even in the best of situations, people's ideals are bound to lose something in the translation. Furthermore, the lure of worldly success often tempts people into really *bad* compromises. Thus when people "sell low," their spiritual ideals may easily devolve into cheap parodies of themselves. On the other hand, if they are unwilling to play the game at all, they will never learn what life is about, or develop any real mobility or confidence in the world.

The Mask leads people into the world; it is related to desire and the search for a physical embodiment of the soul's inner vision. The Mask may be embodied in the external personality, or it may be embodied in lovers or significant others. In Jungian terms the Mask can be seen as the anima or animus. It is the luminous image of beauty that is sought in the outside world. Yeats has called it

"the object of desire" and "the idea of the good,"[5] and tells us that
it is formed from the memories of exalted moments in previous
lives. According to Yeats, all of the faculties are formed out of
memory, and the Mask most of all. Through the Mask the past is
projected into the future; through the Mask people try to to relive
the idealized memories of their best experiences.

The Mask is most commonly associated with sexual and
romantic ideals. However it may also be seen as the *artistic muse*.
Artists use their relationships as sources of inspiration. However,
they realize that the ideality they find in their relationships belongs
neither to themselves nor their lovers. There is often a certain
obliqueness to their relationships—an unwillingness to look too
closely at something that could easily evaporate. Artists approach
life as drama. They know enough to remember that it's a play, but
they also have enough passion to put on a good performance.

The Creative Mind

The Creative Mind is strongest in the third quarter, which extends
from the full Moon (Phase 15), to the waning square (Phase 22).

During the first and second quarters the spirit was descending
into matter; it was taking on a physical form in order to gain
agility, power, and expressiveness within the material world. By
the full Moon this process is complete. Phase 15 is a Virgo phase,
symbolically related to the harvest. The spiritual qualities that
were being developed are now in their final form; they have come
to fruition. Becoming has given way to being, and the questions of
youth—the questions of achievement and growth—have been
replaced by the existential crises of middle age.

Individuals born at the full Moon are closely identified with
their bodies. As the Moon begins to wane, however, physical
vitality also wanes. They become aware of physical decay—not
merely as an abstraction, but as a reality as unavoidable as the
bathroom mirror. Disturbed by the prospect of physical
deterioration and eventual death, they begin to look around for
something incorruptible to identify with. Reversing the habits of a
lifetime, they begin to withdraw the soul from the body, and re-
center themselves within the realms of the Mind and Spirit. It is the
Creative Mind that effects this change, that rescues the soul from its
hypnotic bondage to matter, and turns it back towards its own
immortal source.

Yeats tells us that the Creative Mind is formed from memories of ideas or universals, as represented by actual men and women in past lives. If we remove the reincarnational trappings this statement becomes clearer. Since ideas and ideals are immortal, the great personages of history are also immortal, at least to the degree that they have succeeded in embodying some immortal idea.

For most people the Creative Mind finds its expression in orthodox religions inherited from their parents. By identifying with the immortal ideals of their religion, they are reassured that at least in some measure they will survive physical death. This is only partially true. With the Creative Mind it is not enough to imitate the truth or to worship it. One must participate in it, and become one with it. As the gnostic *Gospel of Philip* says, "Those who say they will die first and then rise are in error. If they do not first receive the resurrection while they live, when they die they will receive nothing."[6] In other words, if the mind is not alive to the truth during this life, then it will not attain the truth in the next life either.

The Creative Mind is keynoted by Phase 15, ruled by the sign Virgo. Negatively, Virgo is a sign rife with assumptions and prejudices. Positively, it gives the curiosity and humility to really communicate with other people, to sift through a million facts and revise opinions accordingly. The difference between the positive and negative Virgo is profound; it is the difference between a petty bigot and an educated humanitarian.

The Creative Mind is akin to the developed Virgoan intellect in that it is an amalgamation or synthesis of many different points of view—of many different truths taken from various cultures, religions, and mythologies. The Creative mind takes an active and partisan approach to intellectual issues. It awakens the mind to the role of ideas and ideals in shaping the world, uncovering many different ways of looking at reality, and showing how each 'operant myth' tends to shape a different reality.

Since the realm of the spirit is immortal, any philosophy that has penetrated into that realm is also immortal, and will crop up repeatedly in the course of human history—merging, expanding, receding, and re-emerging. No religion or philosophy has ever really died. The Egyptian religion still hides within the Cabala; Mithraism lives within Christianity, and Stoicism exists within scientific rationalism. All of these philosophies are available to the intellectual; they are a matter of personal choice, and even personal taste. But it is history that makes the final choice between competing philosophies, for the Creative Mind is a transpersonal force, and for all our foolish ideology, it still manages to operate as a whole, pushing us fitfully towards our higher goals.

The Creative Mind is partly intellectual in nature, but it also has a spiritual component, which may be compared to the Logos or Christ spirit. In this sense it can be seen as the faculty that rescues the soul from its hypnotic bondage to a rigidly materialistic view of reality, and starts opening it up to a more spiritual perspective. Through Knowledge, the Creative Mind frees the soul from the ignorance that keeps it in bondage to the world and the worldly powers.

Now religion may deal with the inner side of this problem— the bondage of sensuality, materialism, and greed, but it carefully sidesteps the 'devil's' outer face—which is the soul's bondage to the State. The State is the most important of the worldly powers, and is directly responsible for most of the world's physical, intellectual, and spiritual repression. Since orthodox religion is usually allied with the State, its truth must be combined with lies, for the unadulterated truth—the integrated truth—is always too radical and controversial to be acceptable to the ruling Powers.

The Creative Mask is penetrating in its social analysis. It looks beyond the facade of society, beyond its hypnotic Mask, to its actual behavior, and the intellectual and philosophical assumptions that underlie that behavior. Society's cultural mythology is criticized and discussed. Its political history is traced. Competing viewpoints are unearthed, assessed, tried on for size. A new intellectual and spiritual synthesis is created, a new model of reality, which is both more comprehensive and more accurate than the old one.

At the full Moon the spirit makes its fullest descent into matter. This is the point of greatest depth; it is the entrance to the underworld, the realm of dreams and imagination. As a Virgo-point it is related to nature and the memory of nature—what Jung calls the collective unconscious. The Creative Mind, which is born at this point, can be seen as a passage of archetypes from the underworld of the racial subconscious, to the the upper realms of individual consciousness. Through the Creative Mind people are 'possessed' or obsessed by living archetypes which give meaning and direction to their otherwise petty and ephemeral existences. Negatively, this possession is by chthonic powers which bind people to the Earth. Positively, their souls are joined to the Mercurial Logos, which liberates them from their earthly prison by guiding them into the immortal realm of the spirit.

By injecting new spiritual archetypes into people's consciousness, the Creative Mind transforms and renews the world. Using Yeats' terminology, the Creative Mind is like the Great Memory of Nature, which acts through the racial memory of humanity by resurrecting, from amidst the vast pantheon of archetypes, those relevant few that will help humanity restore the balance of its world.

The Body of Fate

The Body of Fate is the dominant faculty of the fourth quarter (Phases 22-28). Yeats tells us that the Body of Fate is a series of events seemingly forced on people by the outside world, but actually shaped from memories of unresolved events in past lives. This seems clear enough. However, a study of Phases 21 and 22 reveals that the Body of Fate is not simply karma, not, at least, as it is generally understood.

Phase 21, which immediately precedes the fourth quarter, is symbolized by a besieged cathedral with a shattered rose window. This is a symbol of historical karma if there ever was one. It is a situation that has been repeated throughout history—an old religion or worldview is being attacked by an aggressive new one. The violence of this situation (and the violence of the waning square) represents the inevitable conflict between the old and the new, the past and the future.

Phase 22 is symbolized by a Chinese sage walking nonchalantly through a carnival. As we enter the fourth quarter, our attitude towards life changes completely. We are no longer holding on to a coherent mental schema. The tower has fallen; the rose window has been shattered, and we are surrounded by fragments of ideas and philosophies from the previous quarter. I am reminded of one of Yeats' more obscure quotes: "The Body of Fate is the sum not the unity, of fact, fact as it affects a particular man."[7]

In the last quarter it is necessary to gather together the elements from which the seed of the new cycle will be formed. Yet this is a period of decline and decay, and the path is littered with debris. The new and the vital is mixed with the tawdry and outmoded, and it will take people of wisdom and discrimination to make the distinction—to recognize what is part of their spiritual dharma and what is merely distracting or cumbersome.

The Body of Fate is generally experienced as a part of the outer world. For while it is actually a psychic faculty, it is so completely embedded in the historical situation that it is difficult to differentiate from it. It is not, however, completely outside the sphere of individual control. People master their fates through the *attitudes* they adopt towards their situations, and the paths they take to reach their goals. Maneuverability is also important, since it multiplies people's opportunities for concrete learning experiences.

Since the Capricorn and Aquarius phases are in the fourth quarter, it is not surprising to find a practical, Saturnine streak in the Body of Fate. Through planning, perseverance, and hard work, people of the fourth quarter attempt to find their way to a key position within their world. If they are successful, they will greatly

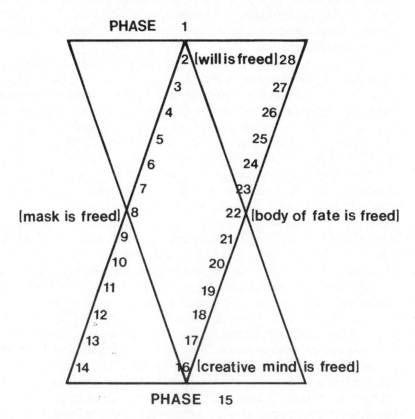

Figure 32.4 Yeat's Intersecting Cones, and the Four Faculties

multiply their opportunities, and their effectiveness in shaping the wider framework of reality.

Because of its position at the end of the cycle, the Body of Fate has a certain sacrificial element. Negatively the call for personal sacrifice is rejected, only to come back in a sense of persecution or fatality. Positively there is a willingness to forgo personal comfort for the good of society. The karma of the Body of Fate is thus chosen rather than enforced. It is not a karma of punishment, but a karma of *commitment*.

Since I based my definitions of the faculties on a study of their zones of influence, one may reasonably ask whether they have an existence independent of the lunar cycle—whether, in fact, there is any point in studying them at all. I myself would not be convinced if it weren't for the fact that every phase in Yeats' system can be derived from a complex interrelationship between the four faculties. This system is so complicated, and so mechanically precise, that it is hard to see how it could work if the faculties had no independent existence.

The movement of the four faculties along two interpentrating cones forms the "Great Symbol" of Yeats' system. It is difficult to visualize, but it's worth the effort. The bases of the two cones represent Phases 1 and 15—the spiritual and material worlds. The faculties move back and forth along the cones in pairs: the Will tied to the Creative Mind, and the Mask to the Body of Fate. (See Figure 32.5.)

The Will of the Moon phase is represented by the phase itself. This is where we are centered, and where we feel our real purpose in life. The Mask, not surprisingly, is represented by the phase opposite the Will. It is the reflection of the Will. Thus, the Mask of Phase 28, the third Aquarius phase, is Phase 14, the third Leo phase.

Finding the Creative Mind is a little more difficult. Remember that the Creative Mind is always paired with the Will; it is reflected across the vertical axis of symmetry, formed by Phases 1 and 15. Thus, if the Will is a waxing phase, the Creative Mind will be a waning phase, and vice versa.

To find the phase of the Creative Mind, first determine how many phases away from Phases 1 or 15 the Will is, and then count the same number of phases on the other side. For instance, when the Will is Phase 24, it is five phases from Phase 1 on the waning side (28, 27, 26, 25, 24). The Creative Mind, then, is found at Phase 6 which is five signs away from Phase 1 on the waning side (2, 3, 4, 5, 6).

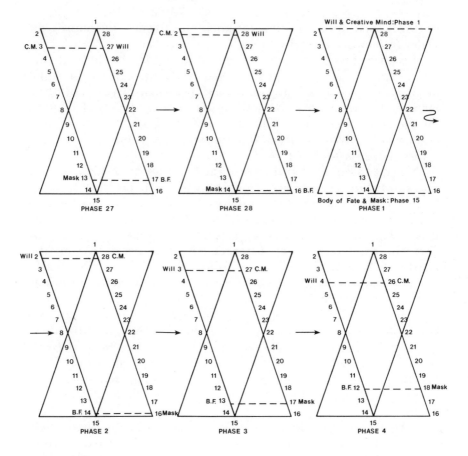

Figure 32.5 Passage from Phase 27 to Phase 4 Along the Inter-penetrating Cones

The Mask of Phase 24 is found at Phase 10, which is the opposite phase in the circle. The Mask is easy to find if one simply identifies the zodiacal sign of the Moon phase and then thinks of the opposite zodical sign. Phase 24, for instance, is the central Capricorn phase, so the Mask of Phase 24 would be Phase 10, the central Cancer phase.

In finding the Body of Fate, remember that it is tied to the Mask; it is a reflection of the Mask across the vertical axis of symmetry. Count the number of phases between the Mask and Phases 1 or 15, and then count the same number of phases on the other side of the cone. Since Phase 10 is five signs from Phase 15

FIGURE 32.6

PHASE #	WILL	MASK	CREATIVE MIND	BODY OF FATE
1	1	15	1	15
2	2	16	28	14
3	3	17	27	13
4	4	18	26	12
5	5	19	25	11
6	6	20	24	10
7	7	21	23	9
8	8	22	22	8
9	9	23	21	7
10	10	24	20	6
11	11	25	19	5
12	12	26	18	4
13	13	27	17	3
14	14	28	16	2
15	15	1	15	1
16	16	2	14	28
17	17	3	13	27
18	18	4	12	26
19	19	5	11	25
20	20	6	10	24
21	21	7	9	23
22	22	8	8	22
23	23	9	7	21
24	24	10	6	20
25	25	11	5	19
26	26	12	4	18
27	27	13	3	17
28	28	14	2	16

(11, 12, 13, 14, 15), the Body of Fate will be five signs away from 15 on the waning side (16, 17, 18, 19, 20). So the Body of Fate is at Phase 20. Notice that the Body of Fate, which is the second Scorpio phase, is opposite the Creative Mind, which is the second Taurus phase.

Yes, I know, it's complicated. But don't worry; Figure 32.6 puts it all down in black and white.

So what good is all of this? Well, in a way it only elaborates the nature of the phases themselves. After all, the Mask of Phase 24 is always Phase 10, its Creative Mind is always Phase 6, and its Body of Fate is always Phase 20. Still, by looking at the faculties we can usually get a better understanding of some of the more contradictory aspects of the phases. For instance, the Body of Fate for Phase 17, which is a sexual phase, is Phase 27, which is renunciatory. Thus, the 'fate' (or the subconscious choice) of the Phase 17 individual is to constantly renounce or lose the objects of desire.

The Body of Fate for Phase 23, which is a rather conservative Capricorn phase, is Phase 21, the besieged cathedral. Thus, while the Will of Phase 23 is to preserve the past, its 'fate' is to see the past being attacked and destroyed on all sides.

In Phases 8 and 22, the Will and the Body of Fate are the same. So at these points in the cycle we can forge our own destiny; Will and Fate are in harmony.

The Mask of Phase 12, the first Leo phase, is Phase 26, the first Aquarius phase. Despite Leonine desires for popularity, we put on a Mask that proclaims we are really quite independent and have little concern for what other people think of us. It is interesting to note that the Mask is always the opposite sign of the Moon phase. Therefore, it can be seen as a form of compensation, an attempt to round out the personality with qualities that are naturally lacking.

The Creative Mind of Phase 12 is Phase 18, the third Libra phase. So, in conjunction with the rather self-serving ambitions of the Leo phase, we find an exalted and idealistic Libran philosophy.

Well, hopefully you get the idea. Just look up your own phase and figure out what its Mask, Creative Mind, and Body of Fate are. Then turn to those phases, and try to see how they apply to your life.

Just a few interpretive guidelines: The Mask tells you something about your 'ideal other,' and also something about what you try to project in your personality. The Creative Mind reveals something about your thought processes, your ideals, and your philosophical beliefs, and what kind of people you emulate. The Body of Fate reveals something about your sense of duty, responsibility, or fate. It may also show something about your politics and social ambitions.

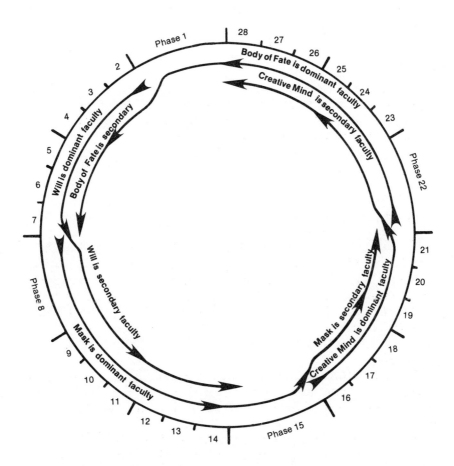

Figure 32.7 Dominant and Secondary Faculties

Notes

1. Paul Foster Case, *The Tarot: the Key to the Wisdom of the Ages* (Richmond, VA: Macoy Publishing Co., 1947), p. 118.

2. Ibid., p. 122.

3. W. B. Yeats, *A Vision* (New York: Macmillan Co., 1969), p. 83.

4. Ibid., p. 192.

5. Ibid.

6. James M. Robinson, gen. ed., *The Nag Hammadi Library*, trans. by Wesley W. Isenbert (Leiden: E. J. Brill, 1977), p. 144.

7. Yeats, p. 82.

Chapter Thirtythree

Energy Flow in the Individual Chart

The Nodes of the Moon turn the flat circle of the chart into an upward or downward moving spiral. Even if we are content to travel in familiar circles, the Nodes bring in transpersonal forces that push us towards evolution or towards degeneration. The North Node beckons us to evolve, and provides us with the spiritual energy to do so, while the South Node tempts us to regress into a more primitive state of mental organization. If there is to be spiritual health, the North Node must dominate.

The chart is like a machine designed for a specific evolutionary task. Locked within the angle between the Sun and the Moon is a unique perspective or point of view, and locked within the planetary pattern is an individual way of approaching life. New Age philosophy notwithstanding, the process of individuation does not give us complete freedom to become anything we want. There are inner laws built right into the chart, and we either abide by them, or we get stuck in our development.

Lunar Subphases

To gain a clearer understanding of energy flow in the chart, we must look in particular to the North Node of the Moon, for this is our tap into the unlimited energy of the cosmos; this is what drives the chart.

The North Node of the Moon sets up a subcycle of Moon phases within the chart, much as the ascendant of the chart sets up a cycle of houses. The lunar subphases backdrop every planet and point in the chart with a specific Moon phase, and consequently, with a secondary zodiacal sign. This information can provide important new insights in chart analysis.

Finding the lunar subphases is very simple. The first lunar subphase spans the area from the North Node of the Moon to 30 degrees past the North Node, while the fifteenth lunar subphase begins at the South Node of the Moon and extends to 30 degrees past the South Node. All the other phases follow just as they would in Figure 3.1. The North Node of the Moon has simply been substituted for the new Moon point.

Let's take a look at the lunar subphases in Walt Disney's chart (Figure 33.1). The ring outside the chart is numbered from 1 to 28, indicating the lunar subphases. You will also notice that subphase 1 begins at the North Node point.

To use the subphases in chart interpretation a little creativity is required. The basic idea is that every planet takes on some of the coloration of the subphase in which it is found. Thus, since Walt Disney's Mercury is in subphase 1, his intellect would tend to be innocent, child-like, and imaginative—even though Mercury is in Scorpio. Mercury in a Piscean Moon phase tends to mellow out the caustic seriousness of Mercury in Scorpio, while at the same time accentuating its natural wit and humor.

What about Disney's overall Moon phase? Since the Moon is waning and there is an angle of 62 degrees between the Sun and the Moon, he is in the very end of Phase 22, which is the imaginative, exploratory Jupiter in Sagittarius phase. However, he is about to progress into Phase 23, the Saturn in Capricorn phase. This cuspal factor is shown clearly by the fact that Disney's mental talents were eventually used to build the solid financial empire of Disneyland, which even had its own Capricornian castle.

Before going on to the subphases, I would like to emphasize that every factor in the chart, including the subphases, must be subordinated to the overall Moon phase, since this defines the individual's basic consciousness and perspective.

The most important subphase in a chart is the one that backdrops the Sun. In Walt Disney's chart this is subphase 2, since the Sun is on the thirteenth degree of Sagittarius, which is 31 degrees ahead of the North Node. Phase 2 is an Aries subphase, associated with a creative, humorous, and child-like mind, that is

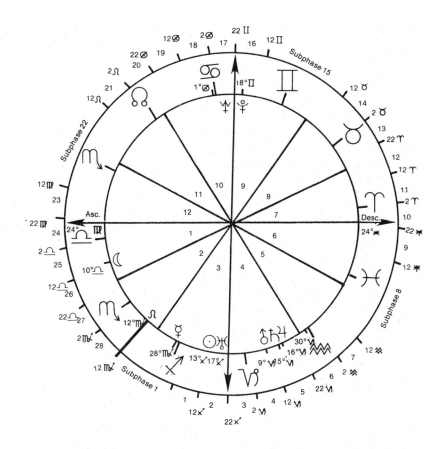

Figure 33.1 Walt Disney's Natal Chart

given to all kinds of mental tricks and manipulations. This helps to explain the exact quality of Disney's solar energies—beyond the fact that he was a Sagittarius, and was thus given to adventure and flights of fancy. Also note that Phase 2 has something of the Sorcerer's Apprentice in it, a characterization that would seem to fit Disney himself. The cartoon of that name will also be remembered as one of his best.

Disney's Moon is on the tenth degree of Libra, which is 32 degrees behind the North Node. This puts his Moon in subphase 25, the last Capricorn phase. Phase 25 is wise, teacherly, and compassionate, and is always looking towards the deeper meaning of human events. Individuals with a strong Phase 25 influence are often spokespeople for a group or collectivity, much as Disney's cartoons served as ambassadors of American thought and culture. One of the highest qualities of Phase 25 is the desire for world peace. The Moon in Libra re-emphasizes this quality in Disney's chart, and we see it amply manifested in his many movies promoting international good will.

The ascendant in Walt Disney's chart is the twenty-fourth degree of Virgo, whose Sabian symbol is "a book for children pictures Mary and her little lamb." Twenty-four Virgo is 48 degrees behind the North Node, putting it in subphase 24. My image for Phase 24 shows a magical rabbit running around a tree. The imagery here is practically repetitive; Phase 24 is a phase of magic, and twenty-four Virgo is storybook land. What Disney was embodying for the world (Ascendant) was the magical realm of the child's imagination.

Notice that most of Disney's planets are found in the first quarter following the North Node, that is, in subphases 1 through 7. This re-emphasizes Disney's preoccupation with issues of early childhood development. The conjunction of Jupiter and Saturn in Capricorn shows a great concern with moral development. The fact that these planets are in subphase 5, a phase of adolescent romanticism, indicates that the keystone of Disney's moral system may have centered on old-fashioned ideas about love, romance, and marriage.

The subphases add many new dimensions to chart interpretation. In using the subphases, everything that has been said about the Moon phases in general can also be applied to the individual chart. For instance, all the planets in the hemicycle following the North Node should be seen as planets of individuation and incarnation. They are planets that the individual must learn to put into action and expression. By contrast, the planets that follow the South Node should be seen as planets of reflection and consciousness expansion. They are planets that are used to aid the individual's creative thought and overall comprehension of life.

The Nodes of the Moon also relate the planets in a person's chart to the four faculties. Thus, any planet in the ninety degrees immediately following the North Node will have a strongly willful quality. Even a planet like Venus will show a strongly willful quality when it is placed in this quadrant. Love will be sought out with determination and resolve, rather than passively awaiting fulfillment.

Planets in the second quarter past the North Node will have a visionary quality and add to the strength of the personality. They will take on the qualities of the Mask. Planets in the third quarter will possess the turbulent thoughtfulness of the Creative Mind, and planets in the fourth quarter will be active in expanding the individual's frame of reference or world-view.

The subphase theory also yields interesting insights into the energy flow of the chart. Using this system the two basic energy streams of the chart can be found by simply locating the North and South Nodes. At first glance this knowledge may seem academic, but in reality it provides the first step to a much deeper and more coherent interpretation of the chart.

Subphases and the Chakras

As has already been observed, the two "active" faculties of the chart—the Will and the Creative Mind—are practically identical with the Pingala and the Ida, which are two major psychic currents of the human body. Assuming that this similarity is not coincidental, we can probably benefit by taking a closer look. Specifically, we may be able to find a correlation between the subphases and the chakras.

Chakras are energy centers in the "etheric" or spiritual body. They are generally located close to the great nerve plexuses of the spinal cord. The most well known of the chakras is the "third eye," which is associated with the power of clairvoyance. All of the chakras are pierced by both the Ida and the Pingala. In fact, one could say that the chakras are created wherever the Ida and Pingala intersect.

Unfortunately, this makes the analogy of the chakras to the subphases somewhat problematic, for the astrological chart is a circle, while the energy pathways of the body are serpentine in form. But to continue our experiment, let us assume that the intertwining serpents of the etheric body are really just a twisted form of the circle. If the analogy is going to hold then the chakras in the astrological chart would have to be composed of at least two subphases—one dominated by the Will or Pingala, and the other dominated by the Creative Mind or Ida. Since it is the Nodal axis that divides the Idic and Pingalic sides of the chart, it is possible that the nodal axis is in some way related to the spinal cord, and that the pairing of subphases occurs across this nodal axis. (See Figure 33.2 for clarification.)

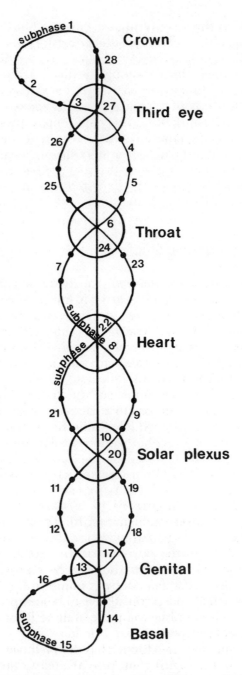

Figure 33.2 Chakras in Relation to the Moon Phases, Helical Form

At this point it becomes a lot easier to figure out the relationship of the chakras to the subphases. First of all, it is obvious that subphases 1 and 15 have a special relationship to the energy flow in the chart, since it is in these phases that the Will and the Creative Mind have their origins. Only two chakras of the human body have this same relationship to the Ida and Pingala: the crown chakra and the basal chakra. Since Phase 15 is associated with the material world, it is a safe bet that subphase 15 is the one related to the basal chakra, while the more spiritually-oriented subphase 1 would be the crown chakra. There are other clues which seem to confirm this hypothesis. The crown chakra, like the North Node, represents an entrance for transpersonal spiritual energies. Furthermore, the visual symbol I came up with for Phase 1 includes a water lily. This conforms closely to the thousand-petaled lotus used by Indian occultists to symbolize the crown chakra.

The relation of subphase 15 to the basal chakra is harder to fathom, especially since Phase 15 is hardly what one would call primitive. However, there are indications. First of all, Phase 15 is related to the material world. Secondly, Phase 15 is survival-oriented, or at least it is concerned with progressing beyond survival values and onto a higher plane of living. One sees another interesting clue in the fact that the South Node of the Moon, which begins subphase 15, is symbolized by an upside down Leo symbol. This symbol can be seen prominently displayed on the hood of the king cobra. In India, the king cobra is the symbol for the kundalini power, which is thought to reside within the basal chakra.

If subphases 1 and 15 represent the crown chakra and the basal chakra, then the positions of the other chakras follow automatically. (See Figure 33.3.) The system is actually quite satisfactory. For instance, at the third eye level we find the Aries subphases and the Aquarius subphases. The Aquarius subphases are, in fact, highly clairvoyant, while the Aries subphases are visual in orientation. This pattern seems to be repeated thoughout the whole system. While the waxing subphases are concerned with physical activities and physical senses, waning subphases on the same chakra level are viewing these same activities and senses from a more internal perspective.

For instance, at the throat chakra level, we find the Taurus subphases on the waxing or pingalic side, and the Capricorn subphases on the waning or idic side. The Taurus phases are

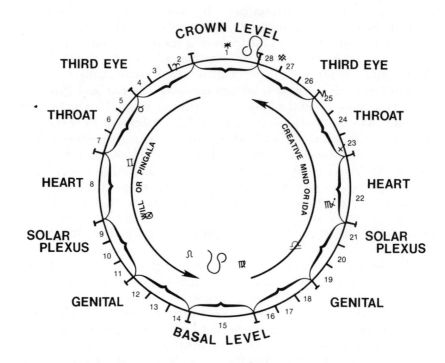

Figure 33.3 Chakras in Relation to the Moon Phases, Circular Form

concerned with coming to grips with life, and achieving a practical and experiential understanding of the world. They are also related to the senses of touch and hearing. By contrast, the Capricorn phases deal with the *inner* side of hearing and touch. Thus, Capricorn phase individuals are successful in their quest for knowledge largely because they can *feel* when an idea is solid and when it is not. They also have an ability to more or less "hear" what other people are thinking, simply by listening to the inner side of what is being said.

One question that remains unanswered is how the circle of the astrological chart can be translated into the serpentine pattern of the etheric body. I can only guess. Perhaps in an unevolved person planetary energies actually *do* run in a circular path. However, with the entrance of *spiritual will*, the energies are in some way redirected or twisted according to the individual's higher purpose. I am reminded once more of Hermes and the caduceus. Coming upon two serpents locked in combat, Hermes struck the ground with his staff, whereupon the serpents twined up the staff to form the caduceus. In much the same way, the spiritual will, operating through the nodal axis, might be able to transform the chaos of the astrological chart into something with a unified purpose and mode of operation.

If the energies represented by the subphases actually do coil around the spinal cord, then it is most probable that the Will and the Creative Mind cross each other at several specific points, and that these points are where the actual chakras are located. Thus, certain pairs of subphases, reflected across the Nodal axis, would form the chakras themselves, while the remaining subphases would form the serpentine pathways connecting the chakras.

Once this possibility was granted, locating the subphases that contain the chakras was easy. Since the chakras are radiant centers depicted by Indian occultists as flowers, I simply looked for the phases with circular or radiant imagery. I noticed immediately that the central phase of each zodiacal sign almost always has circular or radiant imagery. Phase 20, the central Scorpio phase, actually has a flower in it; the central Leo phase features the Sun; the central Cancer phase shows a circular building on a mountaintop; the central Aquarius phase shows an egg, etc. Figure 33.4 shows the completed system.

Tentative though it may be, the correlation of the subphases to the chakras has many implications. The most interesting possibility lies in the field of medical astrology. In fact, this theory may provide the starting point for an entirely new type of medical astrology, based on a correlation between problem areas in the chart and the psychic centers of the body.

The Moon Phases as an Aid to the Study of History

One of the more attractive spin-offs of the Moon phases is their use as a time line. Yeats presented one attempt at such a system in *A Vision*. However, his divisions were so arbitrary and irregular, that they were totally unconvincing. I tried my own hand at it, with no real conviction that it would or even *should* work. After all, why should the Moon phases apply to a larger cycle?

In my first attempt, I began the Piscean Age at Christ's birth, in 7 B.C. A true believer in the sixties, I began the Aquarian Age in

1967. I then divided this span of time into 12 equal divisions, to indicate the major shifts of sign within the Age. Then, I divided all but the mutable signs into three equal sections, in order to account for the divisions of the shorter phases.

What I came up with wasn't all that impressive, but a few things did stick out. Phase 16, which is a phase thickly populated by leaders of various spiritual movements, coincided roughly with the first Crusade. And the Aquarian phases began somewhere around the American revolution. With these facts in hand, I re-drew my time line so that the first Crusade began exactly at Phase 16 and the American Revolution began exactly at Phase 26 (the first Aquarian phase). This, of course, changed both ends of the scale. The Age now began a good deal earlier than Christ's birth. This was just as well, since I had already been chided by a friend concerning the brevity of my Piscean Age. "It *has* to coincide with the astronomically determined length of the age; that's basic!"

The new time line was much more interesting; it was revised backwards and forwards a bit, but eventually settled around certain key dates. There are some real problems, but what it explains, it explains well. There seems to be some kind of intercalary period around the Virgo phase. Something of the sort would have to happen in any case, for the phases are otherwise too small to account for the length of the Age, as determined by astronomical precession. Even with an intercalary phase it is off by about thirty years. I could have fudged my dates, and made specious but convincing explanations about my elegant new time line. However, this version worked so well for the last few hundred years, that it would take a lot of persuading to make me change it. (See Figure 33.4 opposite page.)

The most impressive thing about the time line is what it shows about the zodiacal character of the last few hundred years. The Scorpio phases, for instance, coincide with the proliferation of religious orders and heretical sects. This was the period of the flagellants and of the Great Plague. Christianity began to fall apart, with the exaltation of Aristotelian logic, and later, with the great schism in the Church. Interestingly enough, the Great Schism occurred soon after the beginning of Phase 21, which is symbolized by a cathedral with a broken rose window.

The entire Renaissance fell within the Sagittarian phase. This was an age of vastly expanded mental freedom, and of philosophical and theological speculation. It was also the Age of Exploration.

Figure 33.4: Astrological Time Line

BEGINNING OF AGE	-179	Phase 1:	1st decan Neptune, Uranus
Pisces phase..........................	-122	Phase 1:	2nd decan Jupiter, Sun
(179 B.C. -7 B.C.)	-64	Phase 1:	3rd decan Moon, Neptune
	-7	Phase 2:	Mercury
Aries phases..........................	51	Phase 3:	Sun
(7 B.C. -166 A.D.)	108	Phase 4:	Moon, Mars
	166	Phase 5:	Venus
Taurus phases......................	223	Phase 6:	Mars, Saturn
(166-338 A.D.)	281	Phase 7:	Mars
	338	Phase 8:	1st decan Mercury
Gemini phase.......................	396	Phase 8:	2nd decan Venus
(338-511)	453	Phase 8:	3rd decan Uranus
	511	Phase 9:	Moon
Cancer phases......................	568	Phase 10:	Saturn
(511-683)	626	Phase 11:	Venus, Neptune
	683	Phase 12:	Mars, Pluto
Leo phases...........................	741	Phase 13:	Sun
(683-856)	798	Phase 14:	Mars, Sun
	856	Phase 15:	1st decan Mercury
Virgo phase	913	Phase 15:	2nd decan?
(856-1086??)	971	Phase 15:	2nd decan?
	1028	Phase 15:	3rd decan
	1086	Phase 16:	Jupiter, Saturn
Libra phases.........................	1143	Phase 17:	Pluto, Moon
(1086-1258)	1201	Phase 18:	Sun, Venus
	1258	Phase 19:	Pluto
Scorpio phases	1316	Phase 20:	Neptune, Mars
(1258-1431)	1373	Phase 21:	Moon, Uranus
	1431	Phase 22:	1st decan Mars
Sagittarius phase..................	1488	Phase22:	2nd decan Sun
(1431-1603)	1546	Phase 22:	3rd decan Jupiter
	1603	Phase 23:	Saturn
Capricorn phases..................	1661	Phase 24:	Uranus, Venus
(1603-1776)	1718	Phase 25:	Saturn
	1776	Phase 26:	Uranus
Aquarius phases....................	1833	Phase 27:	Neptune, Venus
(1776-1984)	1891	Phase 28:	Pluto, Saturn
	1948	Phase 1:	1st decan Neptune
Pisces phase	2006	Phase 1:	2nd decan Jupiter, Sun
(1948-2121)	2063	Phase 1:	3rd decan Moon, Neptune

Figure 33.4

The Capricorn phases began inauspiciously with the witchhunts, and the accession of the Presbyterian king, James I, to the throne of England. The difference between the Age of Elizabeth and the Age of James can practically be defined as the difference between Sagittarius and Capricorn.

The whole problem of the "shadow" was hashed out in the Capricorn phases. This was an age of terrible religious wars (including the Thirty Years War), but it was also the period when

England abolished torture, and ended the witchhunts. As part of the flight from superstition, one also saw the birth of mechanistic science, and the rejection of astrology, magic, and Neoplatonic philosophy. The last Capricorn phase brought the Enlightenment, with its worship of objectivity and reason.

The Aquarian phases began abruptly with the American and French Revolutions. This was the beginning of the modern era, characterized by a rapid acceleration of scientific, technological, and medical progress. It was also a period of social dislocation and political modernization. Democracies were instituted in many nations, though there was also a rise of *ideological* dictatorships.

The Moon phases as a backdrop to history tell us little about specific events, but they do tell us a great deal about the spiritual complexion of each period, and the issues that were being dealt with. As with the phases themselves, the changes of zodiacal sign show up most clearly. However, an understanding of the phases themselves—and of their symbols—can also yield interesting insights into each period.

Since the division of the ages into Moon phases seems to work, there is a temptation to prophecize. The next real shift will occur in 2006, when we enter the second decan of Phase 1. This is the most pleasant of the Piscean decans—certainly more pleasant than the first decan, which is rather violent and mentally chaotic. Some kind of spiritual integration is likely to occur during that period; what we are going through now is more in the nature of a spiritual dissolution of the previous age, in preparation for the new synthesis. There is no sense, however, in touting 2006 as the dawn of the Millenium. The Age of Aquarius has already begun, and it has certainly not brought the Millenium. Is it realistic to expect all of humanity's problems to disappear, just because of some event in the heavens?

Moon Phases and the Tarot

Years after I had developed the Moon phase symbols, I realized that a few of the symbols were strikingly similar to tarot cards— the most obvious examples being Phase 25 and Phase 26, which are practically identical to the Hierophant and the Fool. At first I didn't think much of it, but later I tried to assign cards to all the phases. Of course this was pretty much impossible since there are 22 cards in the major arcana and 28 Moon phases.   Yet the correlations were certainly there, so much so that a close study of Paul Foster Case's *The Wisdom of the Tarot* helped me understand the inner dynamics of some of the more difficult phases.

While it is possible that the creators of the tarot cards were tapping into the decan images or Moon phase images, it is unlikely that there was an actual historical connection. The history of the tarot is a foggy one. My own conjecture is that it was a spin-off of medieval Christian memory systems for the virtues and vices. Thus one finds Strength, Temperance, and Justice, as well as other virtues and vices that are almost as clear: the Emperor is Rectitude; the Hanged Man is Compassion; the High Priestess is Wisdom; the Fool is Folly; the Devil is Lust; the Falling Tower is Pride, etc. I will leave you to your own conclusions on this subject. Below are the attributions that I have settled on. Reading Case side by side with my phase descriptions may prove illuminating.

Moon Phase	Tarot Card	Moon Phase	Tarot Card
Phase 1	?	Phase 12	Strength
Phase 2	Magician	Phase 13	Sun
Phase 3	Sun	Phase 14	Temperance
Phase 4	High Priestess	Phase 15	Justice
Phase 5	Empress	Phase 16	Chariot
Phase 6	Emperor	Phase 17	Moon, Devil
Phase 7	?	Phase 18	Judgment
Phase 8	Lovers	Phase 19	High Priestess
Phase 9	Star	Phase 20	Hanged Man
Phase 10	Hermit	Phase 21	Falling Tower
Phase 11	?	Phase 22	World

Moon Phase	Tarot Card	Moon Phase	Tarot Card
Phase 23	Wheel of Fortune	Phase 26	Fool
Phase 24	Devil	Phase 27	Empress (inner side)
Phase 25	Hierophant	Phase 28	Death

The Decanates

When I began my study of the Moon phases, I tried to free my mind from the traditional view of the decanates, for it was clear even at the beginning of my research that these ideas fit the material very poorly. Yet it was also obvious that there was an intrinsic relationship between the Moon phases and the signs of the zodiac. Thus it was impossible for me to ignore the possibility that the smaller, 10-degree phases were indeed associated with the zodiacal decanates.

After I had completed my initial observations on the Moon phases, I tried to construct a new system of decanate rulerships based on the planetary attributions revealed by the research. This attempt was basically unsuccessful. There did seem to be patterns, but nothing that impressive. A neat systematization had not materialized, and I wasn't about to force it.

But as I did more charts I realized that there is, in fact, a strong connection between the decanates and the smaller phases—even if it doesn't follow any easily grasped system of planetary rulerships. People with the Sun in the last decanate of Scorpio actually do seem to show a lot of the characteristics associated with Phase 21, the third Scorpio Phase. And people with the Sun in the second decanate of Cancer actually do show a lot of characteristics of Phase 10, the second Cancer Phase. This may be a useful new approach to understanding the decanates—one which could be both more accurate and more substantive than the traditional system of rulerships.

A word of caution, however. The Moon phases represent a particular cycle, a cycle of germination, growth, maturation, decay, and renewal. In this cycle the youthful and extroverted quality of the early signs is stressed, while the reflective and psychologically complex side of the later signs is emphasized. Thus, if you approach the decanates exclusively through the Moon phases, you will inevitably introduce certain distortions, for the decanates have characteristics which are independent of any particular cycle.

The following is a list of keywords for the smaller Moon phases. I offer it both as a review of the Moon phases and as a description of the characteristics of the decanates. Since the divisions in the larger Moon phases were not analyzed in as much depth, the keywords for the decanates of the mutable signs have been taken directly from Sun sign research.

Keywords for the Decanates as Revealed by the Phases of the Moon

1st Aries Decan: intellectual discovery; spark of genius; reality as defined by words and concepts; power of speech; physical desire; the sorcerer's apprentice; l'enfant terrible; humorous; mischievous or devilish; manipulative.

2nd Aries Decan: goodness and light; spreading a message of peace and brotherhood; solar, radiant, vital, fun-loving; developing independence and self-confidence; developing physical coordination; exploring the world; embodiment of ideals.

3rd Aries Decan: refined analysis of society and culture, using both logic and intuition; social idealism; marshalling of social energies; dualism; moral choice; penetrating perceptivity; decisiveness; battle of good and evil; detached objectivity versus primitive passion; gifts of one's culture.

1st Taurus Decan: emotional outreach; willingness to risk pain for love; blossoming of romantic sentiment; poignancy; vulnerability versus worldly wisdom; ability to draw meaning from experience; reflection, understanding; solidification of human values; experience.

2nd Taurus Decan: desire for freedom; fighting for personal space; uncovering personal and social repressions; attunement to sub-conscious currents; psychoanalysis; rebelliousness (hostility and hate); natural impulses vs. ego control; longing for the simplicity and openness of nature; social justice; re-analysis.

3rd Taurus Decan: tackling collective problems through cooperative interaction; complexity of viewpoint; practical readjustments; potency of action; materialization; accurate appraisal of skills and resources; sublimation of sexual energy into productive work; transforming negative situations; healing.

1st Cancer Decan: attunement to the rhythm and flow of life; finding one's subjective center; unifying power of human emotions; formation of social groups; inclusiveness versus exclusiveness; warmth, generosity, accessiblity; optimism; trusting the life force.

2nd Cancer Decan: isolated intellectual growth; piecing together a comprehensive world-view; conscious mind growing out of unconscious mind; administrative function of the ego; worldly ambition; practical planning; self-programming through attention to unconscious habit patterns.

3rd Cancer Decan: living out a romantic dream; romantic, sentimental; visionary; attunement to the needs of the public; the healing power of love; consequences of illusion and self-deception; home and family; spiritual idealism; power of memory.

1st Leo Decan: leadership; idealistic political movements; mobilization of personal and collective energies; desire for power (misuse of political, sexual or occult energies); self-control; courageous confrontation with opposing forces, or use of devious strategems to achieve selfish ends; grooming oneself for success; power of symbols; propaganda.

2nd Leo Decan: radiant self-expression; full-bodied appreciation of life; development of personal talents; pride; desire for praise; sharing one's courage and energies with others; establishing a family; courageous exploration of life and the world; hunger for life; rounding out and strengthening one's personality.

3rd Leo Decan: living an ideal self-image; seeking a higher unity; spiritual quest; revelation; realizing the purpose for one's manifestation; trials; indomitable will; physical stamina; transformation and sublimation of sexual energy; chivalry.

1st Libra Decan: spiritual awakening; desire to merge with God; religious movements; gathering of spiritual forces (intoxication with potentialities); exploration of the symbolic mind (mental chaos); sublime beauty of the mind; poetry; mythology; sense of historical overview; idealistic re-analysis of history.

2nd Libra Decan: Pluto and Persephone; journey to the underworld (living in a dream world); illusions and unconscious projections; sexual fantasies; temptations of power; decay versus mental and physical self-discipline; finding something incorruptible to believe in; underlying loyalty to ideals; poetic rapture; yoga.

3rd Libra Decan: transcendence; victory of light over darkness; dispassion; fearlessness; mental poise and clarity; sense to of perspective; historical overview; social idealism; the inspiration of beauty; keeping one's relationships on a high plane; the Muses.

1st Scorpio Decan: distrust of the obvious; deception of the senses; penetration to underlying causes; understanding of power; positive and negative uses of political or occult power; moral dialectics; intellectual acumen; persuasiveness; power of words and symbols; metaphysical questions; occultism.

2nd Scorpio Decan: dropping useless ideas and emotions; emotional purification; cynical egotism versus reverent attunement to life; regeneration; centering; regaining perspective; understanding beauty and ugliness; positive and negative culture; complexities of the human condition; opening one's heart to others.

3rd Scorpio Decan: restructuring one's worldview; new spiritual insights which shatter old assumptions; preserving one's cultural heritage; embodying key social values; social conscience; self-sacrifice; political and ideological struggles (confusion and pointless arguments).

1st Capricorn Decan: self-discipline; duty; freeing oneself from paralyzing personal problems (inertia and depression); karma; moral force; uprightness; bringing to life the wisdom of the past; pulling away from the world and back to center; self-application; work; extravagant self-expression.

2nd Capricorn Decan: appreciation of the magical inner forms of nature; mischievous play of occult forces; integrating different facets of the personality, especially those that are demonic or animalistic; material reality as a dream-like illusion; reality as a cultural agreement; dedication to a personal vision of reality; vitalizing society by provoking controversy.

3rd Capricorn Decan: final integration of the personality; character; solid understanding of the deeper aspects of existence (penetration of the mysteries); dispensing wisdom; compassion; emotional depth; sense of identification with and responsibility for the whole of humanity; reverence for life.

1st Aquarius Decan: breaking away from society; getting rid of excess baggage; going where the action is; back to nature movements; following an inner spirit or impulse; utopian idealism; misfits; crazy wisdom; the fool and the genius; instantaneous analysis.

2nd Aquarius Decan: meditation; self-recollection; focusing the inner light; the garden of the soul; mysticism (wrapped up in dreams and illusions); sensual refinement; sweetness, gentleness; spiritual discrimination and balance; ministering to the spiritual needs of others; patience and forbearance; renunciation.

3rd Aquarius Decan: indestructibility of the life force; transformation; death of the old to make way for the new; inalterable cycles of nature; physical laws; social cycles; visionary attunement to the future versus sense of hopelessness (destructive and anti-social behavior); stark realism; willing sacrifice for the future of the race.

Decanate Qualities of the Mutable Signs (taken from Sun-sign data)

1st Gemini Decan: callowness; innocence; emerging individuality; awakening to life's possibilities; making intelligent life decisions despite a lack of adequate information; looking out for one's own interests; compassion or violent dualism; good versus evil.

2nd Gemini Decan: chutzpah; belief in self; courage to enter fully into life; energetic self-projection; joyousness; developing talents; eloquence; opportunities; playing one's cards right.

3rd Gemini Decan: complexity of the Universe; multi-faceted mind; inability of the mind to grasp the whole picture; foolishness and its closeness to wisdom; imagination as a way of revealing reality; detachment; commentary.

1st Virgo Decan: being true to oneself; personal standards; honesty and outspokenness; irrepressible individuality; expressiveness; ability to stand up to social criticism, strong convictions; morality; vulnerability versus self-protection.

2nd Virgo Decan: changing what one can change, and accepting what one can't; inspiring others to stand up to social forces; humanizing society; sensitivity; compassion; natural beauty; art; celebration of personal freedom; sexual self-expression.

3rd Virgo Decan: social analysis and commentary; perfecting the self in order to better serve others; spontaneous self-giving;sense of give and take in relationships; combative honesty; acts as a levelling influence on society; vitalizing new social movements.

1st Sagittarius Decan: living quality of the truth; participation in the dance of life; flux; openness to one's immediate situation; need for new experiences and new approaches to reality; freedom to create one's own world; intuition that goes to the heart of the situation.

2nd Sagittarius Decan: free flow of energy from unconscious to conscious; being at one with one's creative center or daemon; inspiration; genius and madness; play of creative and destructive energies.

3rd Sagittarius Decan: broadminded understanding of the larger situation; overview; perspective on the self; teaching; opening other people's minds; questioning social assumptions; energizing dynamic social movements; moral, philosophical issues; the dance.

1st Pisces Decan: common problems; crazy mixed-up quality of life; serenity in the midst of chaos; surrealism; closeness of life to death; spiritual values; search for meaning; inner beginnings of external events; consequences of one's gestalt; caution (fear); compassionate understanding of other people's situations.

2nd Pisces Decan: awakening from the dream; getting one's bearings; innocent and trusting, but nobody's fool; openness to what life has to offer; conquest of fear; the aura; attracting sympathy and guidance; battle for supremacy between in-group and out-group; personal tap into truth.

3rd Pisces Decan: the timeless soul crucified in time and space; old meets new; sharing one's wisdom with the new generation, but also learning from them; the issues of one's historical period; accessibility; helpful advice; inner nobility.

The Egyptian Decan Symbols in the Western Occult Tradition

The ancient Egyptians divided the ecliptic, or zodiacal belt, into thirty-six minor constellations. By observing which of these constellations rose above the Eastern horizon at dusk, they could determine the approximate time of year. Since there were thirty-six constellations and about 360 days in a year, a new constellation would appear every ten days.

The Egyptians were not very advanced astronomers, however. In fact, their civil calendar lost so much time that they had to introduce a secondary calendar based on the motion of the stars. Unfortunately, by the time they got around to it the decanates had already become totally confused, at least as a method for measuring time. Thus, the number and order of the decanates varies greatly, even in the tombs of the New Kingdom. It appears, in fact, that the decanates had already lost their original function as a method of measuring time, and had become a system of symbolic astrology, used primarily in magic and funerary ritual.

The Egyptians have always had quite a reputation for magic. So, when the Hellenistic Greeks were developing astrology in its "modern" form, they appropriated the Egyptian decan gods in order to give their system more power. In the centuries that followed, the decan gods traveled from Greece, to India, back to the middle East, across Africa, and on to Spain and Italy. Of course, by the time they reached Renaissance Italy, in a book called the *Picatrix,* they had already gone through innumerable transformations, and bore practically no resemblance to the original Egyptian sources. Nonetheless, their Egyptian origin was known, and they were, therefore, considered very powerful. Frances Yates', in her masterwork, *Giordano Bruno and the Hermetic Tradition,* describes the decan tradition as a far from insignificant component of Renaissance thought, commented upon and promoted by such important figures as Marsilio Ficino, Cornelius Agrippa, and Giordano Bruno.

Marsilio Ficino was particularly keen on them. Generally known as the leading Neoplatonist of the Renaissance, Ficino was a leading proponent of the Egyptian wisdom tradition. By translating the *Hermetica,* he started something of an "Egyptian revival" in Europe.[1]

Throughout the Renaissance, the "Egyptian" decans were considered the most powerful elements in astrology, for the decan gods were thought to mediate between the angelic realm and Earth by way of the astrological signs. Ficino himself considered the decans demonic, and drew the line between black and white magic at precisely this point. Others were not so cautious. Cornelius Agrippa promoted them openly in his *De Occulta Philosophia.* In fact, this politically careless espousal of pagan doctrines may be seen as one of many causes for the Protestant Reformation. Luther and his followers were convinced that the Catholic Church, with all of its statues and candles, its holy water and incense, had become corrupted by "Egyptian necromancy."

Before the curtain fell on the Renaissance, however, there was a period of considerable freedom, when artists were able to incorporate the decan images into paintings and woodcuts without fear of retaliation. The most impressive of the artworks remaining to us is the Sala dei Mesi of the Palazzo Schifanoia, in Ferrara. The Sala dei Mesi is a room twenty-five by seventy-five feet, decorated from floor to ceiling with high-Renaissance paintings. The walls are divided into three horizontal bands. The top-most band represents the life of heaven; the bottom-most band represents the life of Earth and more particularly, the life of the court. The central band, mediating between heaven and Earth, shows the astrological decan figures.

Unlike the *Hermetica*, the decan figures actually were of Egyptian origin, though they had gone through innumerable transformations and corruptions before arriving at the Sala dei Mesi. The first decan of Aries, for instance, is symbolized in the Palazzo Schifanoia as a black man with fiery red eyes, dressed in a white robe. This figure was originally the Egyptian god Khonsu, transformed first by Greek astrologers into a hybrid of Khonsu and Perseus, and then by Indian astrologers into an angry Negro holding an axe. The subject is an extremely interesting one. However, the twists and turns of the decan tradition are far beyond the scope of this discussion, and will have to wait for another book.

What surprised me most was how much of this tradition has survived. Unfortunately, the astrological community has almost no knowledge of it, and it remains the province of obscure academic works, like Wilhelm Gundel's *Dekane und Dekansternbilder*, Franz Boll's *Sphaera*, and Otto Neugebauer's *Egyptian Astronomical Texts, Vol. III.* I have made a thorough study of these books, and have compiled a large number of the old decan systems, harking from ancient and Ptolemaic Egypt, Greece, India, Arabic Spain, and Northern Europe. Most of the European systems are essentially useless, since they are corruptions of corruptions of corruptions of Egyptian sources. Not only have the symbols been completely transformed in their twisted journey through Europe, Asia, and Africa, but they have also lost all connection to the mythological substructure of Egyptian religion.

For example, the Palazzo Schifanoia shows the third decan of Taurus as a dark, muscular man, with tusks poking through his lips. These tusks are derived from earlier variants that go back to a Ptolemaic system showing a boar on a pedestal. Unbeknownst to European astrologers, this boar represents the Egyptian god Set, and especially Set as the eater of Osiris' eye. The original symbolism is, therefore, a reference to the *waning Moon*—for Set is the Egyptian god of darkness, and he is eating Osiris' eye, which was equated with the Moon. As if to confirm this interpretation, other decan systems from the Ptolemaic period show the eye of Osiris at this point, or even Osiris himself. None of this can be inferred from the decan symbol in the Palazzo Schifanoia; the tusked man is a striking image, but it is symbolically opaque.

Interestingly enough, I found the systems of the Ptolemaic period to be the most valuable. The earlier systems, which go back to at least 2000 B.C., have little variety from one decan to another, but seem an endless repetition of upright snakes and lion-headed gods. The fact that the Ptolemaic systems are "heavier" on an occult level should not be surprising. Alexandrian Egypt was the breeding ground for most of the important elements of the Western occult tradition—including alchemy, gnosticism, the Hermetica, and the decan gods.

As far as I have unravelled it, the Egyptian astrological system is an extremely *good* one. It is too bad that it is still in the hands of a few academics who are completely hostile to astrology. But this must ultimately be blamed on the astrological community itself, which has allowed the uneducated pronouncements of Cyril Fagan (and Edgar Cayce) to shape its ideas on Egyptian religion and Egyptian astrology. Ironically, all of these fantasies and channelings are in no way as interesting as the *actual* tradition.

But what about the Egyptian decan symbols? Do they have any relationship to my own images for the phases? First of all, I must admit to borrowing a few details from the European decan systems. The most significant addition was in Phase 8. Originally, my image pictured a crowned woman in white, delivering a speech. I added the kneeling gardener and the aristocrat later on, adapting them from a decan image in the Palazzo Schifanoia. The gardener was originally a kneeling Hercules, and the aristocrat, Apollo.

There is certainly very little Egyptian symbolism in my images, which incline, instead, to the medieval. However, on the level of meaning rather than form, one finds significant agreement in most of the phases. For instance, Phase 3, which I have pictured as two children running down a hillside on a sunny day, was pictured in many Egyptian systems as Horus, represented as a child sitting on a lotus. First of all, there are children in both pictures. Secondly, Horus is a solar god, the god of the resurrected spring Sun.

In my system, Phase 5, the first decan of Taurus, was symbolized by a flower peddler. The Egyptians, in *some* lists, show Nefertum, the god of flowers and perfumes. In my symbol for the first Cancer phase, I show a woman playing a guitar by a river, with a large paddlewheeler going by. In the Egyptian lists, this spot is generally reserved for Isis, standing upright in a boat. These are just a few of the many similarities.

The decan symbols of the Egyptian and European occult traditions do, in fact, seem to be distant ancestors of the symbols presented in this book. Although my understanding of these symbols was arrived at through a study of the Moon phases, it may be that I have simply stumbled onto the old decan symbols. If this is the case, it remains for me to come up with three decan images for each of the mutable signs. But that will have to wait.

Note

1. The *Hermetica* is a collection of theosophical treatises that takes the form of dialogues between Egyptian gods. It was mistakenly dated by Ficino and his followers to the time of Moses, but it was actually written in the first three centuries of our era, and represented a late synthesis of Greek and Egyptian thought.

Chapter Thirtyfour

Epilogue: Towards a Lunar Astrology

In interpreting an astrological chart, we take astronomical facts and assign psychological or spiritual meanings to them. The placement of the Sun means one thing, the placement of the Moon another. Primitive astrology is basically a body of correlations going back more than two thousand years. Why then, in the entire history of Western astrology, have the Moon phases received so little attention? The waxing and waning of the Moon is a phenomena so obvious, so mythically suggestive, that it has to be important. Primitive people knew this, yet in modern astrology the Moon phases have been practically dismissed—and more or less relegated to the farmer's almanacs and planting guides. Dane Rudhyar wrote a small book on the subject—a good book—and while astrologers seem to know about it, they don't really use it. Wergin and Busteed's *Phases of the Moon* has received even less attention. It is true that the moon phases are somewhat complex, but so are Arabian parts, Uranian planets, solar arcs, and the rest of the manias of modern astrology. It's not complexity per se that is keeping people away. It's something about the Moon...

Astrology grew up around the solar court. The most famous astrologers served emperors, kings, and nobles. By catering to worldly rulers, astrology betrayed its lunar roots, and eventually lost touch with them. Of course there was also political repression afoot. The lunar roots of astrology are found in ancient Babylon and Egypt. Both cultures had important lunar gods and goddesses that figured prominently in their astrology. Roman astrology was much less spiritualized, and for this very reason it became the dominant form of astrology in the Western world. For only when astrology had become spiritually dessicated was it given a place alongside the dominant Christian culture. The Catholic Church would tolerate astrology, and even use it, as long as it did not compete on a spiritual level.

Early Christianity incorporated elements of many of the other mystery religions of the period, and robbed them of their competitive appeal. The worship of Isis, which was very popular around the time of Christ, was eventually incorporated into Christianity by way of the cult of the Virgin. But Christianity is essentially a solar religion, because Christ is basically a heroic light-giver. Thus, Christianity could never really satisfy the lunar impulse, even with the introduction of a highly ritualized mass, and even with the gradual deification of the Virgin Mary.

In its early years, Catholicism's strongest competition came from Gnosticism. Gnosticism was born in Alexandrian Egypt in the first centuries of the Christian era. By the second and third centuries it was a fairly powerful movement. Gnosticism was a strangely visionary religion borrowing elements from Hebrew, Iranian, Greek, Egyptian, and Christian cosmologies. Since Gnosticism tended to promote an active, experiential approach to religion, there often seemed to be as many variants of Gnosticism as there were Gnostics themselves. However, certain basic beliefs did run through most of the sects. In general, the Gnostics believed that the world was evil, the creation of a Jehovah-like god, who in his arrogance, claimed to be self-created, forgetting that he had actually been created by Sophia, the first emanation of the Godhead. Sophia was a High Priestess or Isis figure. She might also be compared to Eve in that it was her misjudgment that caused the Fall. However, Sophia was an infinitely more exalted figure than Eve. Not only was she incorporeal rather than human, but she was also the mother of the entire creation.

Sophia's 'folly' was that she believed herself capable of giving birth to an image which faithfully replicated the Godhead. Before she knew it, this miscalculation had led to the birth of Yaldabaoth (or Jehovah) and later to the world. Because it was Sophia who had created the world, the primary responsibility for its redemption also fell on her, though this was to be accomplished through a new emanation—the historical Jesus.

Besides making Sophia the highest knowable deity, the Gnostics had other characteristically 'lunar' qualities. One of the main reasons they were so reviled by Catholics was the fact that they allowed women to preach, and even had female bishops. Everyone was believed capable of authentic religious experience. Thus, the hierarchical division between clergy and laity could never really develop. Gnosticism encouraged personal religion; it encouraged visionary and ecstatic states, and the development of poetic and mythic imagination. In other words, Gnosticism encouraged the spiritually receptive side of the lunar principle.

If we look at the Moon card of the tarot, we see a lobster crawling out of the water, and a dog and a wolf howling at the Moon. The basic concept of the card is biological or natural evolution. Lunar religion recognizes that in order for us to evolve spiritually we must start where we are, and then develop according to our own internal patterns. Lunar religion assumes that there will be many transformations along the path of spiritual development. These transformations will be mirrored in an ever-changing stream of psychologically relevant imagery.

Because lunar religion understands something of inner process, it is not likely to allow religious symbolism to crystallize into obstructive doctrine. This is quite different from orthodox Christianity, where the highest relgious states are held up for emulation in the absence of any realistic pathways by which to attain them. This failure is easily understood if one only admits the obvious: that orthodox Christianity is as much an authoritarian system of political control as it is a religion. In both the Catholic and Protestant churches, obedience is the central value—obedience to moral law, obedience to the church, obedience in behavior and obedience in *thought*. Conservative Christians are not taught that Christ-consciousness is attainable. They are taught that they are weak, unworthy, and in need of forgiveness. They are taught to obey. The impulse of Gnosticism was radically different; spiritual knowledge was all-important—knowledge by which to attain personal liberation—not just in the afterlife, but now.

Sensing the growing power of the Gnostic movement, the Catholic Church attempted a compromise. In A.D. 325, the Council of Nicaea incorporated a few Gnostic ideas into Church dogma. It didn't work; Gnosticism continued to exist. In A.D. 389, the Catholic emperor Theodosius had the Alexandrian library burned in order to stamp out 'paganism.' From that point on, the

Gnostics were persecuted into virtual extinction, so much so, that until the recent discovery of the Nag Hammadi library, most of what was known of the Gnostics came from attacks on them by early Church fathers.

So what does a defunct spiritual movement have to do with modern astrology? Plenty. First of all, it's not really defunct. Variants of Gnosticism have cropped up throughout Western history, and where they have gotten a foothold humanity has progressed and prospered. Gnostic philosophy was at the core of the Italian Renaissance. Gnostic philosophy was behind the "Rosicrucian Enlightenment" of the early seventeenth century. Gnostic philosophy was behind the Masons, and by extension, the American and French revolutions. Gnostic philosophy was behind the occult revival of the Victorian Age, and particularly the Golden Dawn. Gnosticism is at the core of Jungian psychology, and many of the New Age philosophies that follow in the wake of Jungian psychology. The 'lunar stream' has been and will always be at the center stage of human evolution. It will always be associated with the occult and it will always be associated with anti-authoritarian political movements.

Given some historical distance, it will eventually be clear that the 'youth rebellion' of the 1960's was a millenarian Gnostic movement well within the tradition of all the Gnostic movements before it. The Counterculture's unbridled utopianism is the real giveaway. The hippies of the '60s genuinely believed that the New Age was at hand. On a political level, they were in open rebellion against the church and the state. They instinctively moved towards the same free-form anarcho-communism that we find in other Gnostic movements. On a sexual level, the Counterculture was essentially libertine, though the ascetic strain found in other Gnostic movements was also present to some degree. Gnosis, or direct knowledge, was sought through the sacramental use of LSD, which, under the right circumstances, can provide direct access to higher spiritual realms.

The emergence of pantheism, animism, and religious eclecticism during the '60s closely mirrored the religious syncretism of the original Gnostics. The old pagan Earth religions also made a strong comeback, not only in the incorporation of traditional American Indian values, but also in a renewed respect for the Earth, the Moon, and the Sun. The worship of the Earth appeared in an enormously expanded ecological consciousness. Solar worship surfaced in the anti-nuclear and solar energy movements. And lunar worship emerged in the feminist movement, the most radical portion of which actually does worship the Moon. Inevitably, astrology also made a strong comeback. With an unfailing 'Gnostic' instinct, astrologers like Jones and Rudhyar, who were rooted in the older occult traditions, drew the most attention, despite the fact that they were often more difficult to read.

But the '60s are over. In 1970, the "me" decades began, and unfortunately, astrology was affected as much as the rest of the culture. The search for occult truth, spiritual growth, and cultural reform was largely replaced by a search for 'fulfilling relationships,' sexual and muscular integration, and promising real estate deals. The astrological scene became broader and a lot friendlier, but it also lost a lot of its depth. Superficial commercial astrologers, at home with the spiritually bankrupt dominant culture, began to move back to the fore. The Gnostic impulse was not lost, but failing to define itself clearly, it became submerged and diluted. Furthermore, as the '60s passed further from view, lunar astrology began to seem increasingly weird to a public that had once more begun to define itself in terms of conformist values. And, of course, there was also the problem of the Moon...

During the Piscean Age, lunar values have been consistently repressed. Women have been consistently repressed, and I am not just talking about pay scales. Throughout much of the Age, women who were independent-minded or overly experimental in their belief systems could be burned as witches. Subtler forms of oppression also permeated the culture. Take astrology. While the Moon is said to rule Cancer, look at the way astrologers describe the Moon in Cancer. It generally comes off sounding like an Irish washerwoman: sympathetic, dumb, and a good little homemaker. Rubbish! Anyone who has done any research on the Moon in Cancer knows that these people are hardly housebound. In fact, they are often world travellers. They are also extremely deep thinkers with a natural leaning towards psychology, occultism, and natural philosophy.

The long-term oppression of women in Western civilization has led to a huge accretion of negative emotions in the collective unconscious. Read some radical feminist literature, where these emotions are actually erupting, to get some idea of what is involved. The fear that people have of the lunar side of the occult is based on a subconscious perception of the dark and turbulent side of the 'repressed feminine.' It is tempting to simply deny these emotions—and most people do just that. But people who are on the spiritual path should know better. The Moon is what connects the higher and lower levels of Being. If we deny our baser emotions we will end up strangling off our higher emotions and perceptions along with them. Our task, like the lobster in the Moon card, is to start where we are and slowly crawl out of the mud. The lunar side of life, the lunar side of astrology, has its perils and temptations. But the Moon is the very soul of astrology, for it is the Moon that actually connects us to planetary energies. Without this direct intuitive experience of planetary energies, astrology is just a game, a manipulation of figures and symbols. Even star-gazing comes closer to astrology's original goal, the goal of cosmic attunement.

From our alienated perspective, the Moon may seem dark and treacherous, but remember that the Moon is at the very core of the evolutionary stream. Trust it, follow it, and you will get where you're going. As for our culture the path is even clearer, for its outline has already been mapped out a dozen times by successive waves of Gnostic Illumination.

Figure 34.1

Bibliography and Recommended Reading

Boll, Franz. *Sphaera.* Leipzig: Druck und Verlag von B. G. Teubner, 1903.

Bouche-Leclercq, A.. *Astrologie Grecque.* Paris: Ernest Leroux, 1899.

Busteed, Marilyn, Richard Tiffany, and Dorothy Wergin. *Phases of the Moon.* Berkeley and London: Shambhala Publications, 1974.

Case, Paul Foster. *The Tarot: the Key to the Wisdom of the Ages.* Richmond, Va.: Macoy Publishing Co., 1947.

Cumont, Franz. *Astrology and Religion Among the Greeks and Romans.* New York: Dover, 1960.

de Rougemont, Denis. *Love in the Western World.* New York: Harper and Row, 1956.

Fortune, Dion. *The Mystical Qabalah.* New York: Ibis Books, 1981.

Gundel, Wilhelm. *Dekane und Dekansternbilder.* Hamburg: J. J. Augustin, 1936.

..... *Neue astrologische Texte des Hermes Trismegistos.* Munchen: Abh. Bayer. Akad. Wiss., 1936.

Hand, Robert. *Essays on Astrology.* Gloucester, Mass.: Para Research, 1989.

Harper, George Mills. *Yeats's Golden Dawn.*New York: Barnes and Noble, 1974.

Jonas, Hans. *The Gnostic Religion.* Boston: Beacon Press, 1963.

Jones, Marc Edmund. *Astrology: How and Why It Works.* New York: Sabian Publishing Society, 1969.

Jones, Marc Edmund. *The Sabian Symbols in Astrology.* Stanwood, Washington: Sabian Publishing Society, 196 .

Klimczak, Rick. *New Foundations in Astrology.* Silver Spring, Md.: Arachni Press, 1983.

Lovejoy, Arthur. *The Great Chain of Being: a Study of the History of an Idea.* Cambridge: Harvard U. Press, 1936.

Neugebauer, Otto, and Richard Parker. *Egyptian Astronomical Texts: Decans, Planets, Constellations, and Zodiacs, Vol.3.* Providence: Brown University Press, 1969.

Pingree, David. "The Indian Iconography of the Decans and Horas," in *Journal of the Warburg and Courtauld Institutes,* XXVI, 1963.

Reed, Ishamel. *Mumbo Jumbo.* New York: Doubleday, 1972.

Robinson, James, gen. ed. *The Nag Hammadi Library.*San Francisco: Harper and Row, 1977.

Rosenthal, M.L., ed. *Selected Poems and Two Plays of William Butler Yeats.* New York: MacMillan, 197O.

Rudhyar, Dane. *Astrological Signs: the Pulse of Life.* Boulder, Colorado: Shambhala, 1978.

...... *The Lunation Cycle*. Netherlands: Servire-Wassenaar, 1967.

Silberer, Herbert. *Hidden Symbolism of Alchemy and the Occult Arts*. New York: Dover Publications, 1971.

Wade, Allan, ed. *The Letters of W.B. Yeats*. London: Rupert Hart-Davis, 1954.

Yates, Frances. *The Art of Memory*.   Chicago: University of Chicago Press.

...... *Giordano Bruno and the Hermetic Tradition*. Chicago: University of Chicago Press, 1964.

...... *The Occult Philosophy in the Elizabethan Age*. London: Ark Paperbacks, 1983.

...... *The Rosicrucian Enlightenment*. Boulder, Colorado: Shambhala, 1978.

Yeats, William Butler. *The Celtic Twilight*. Gerrards Cross: Colin Smythe, 1981.

...... *Essays and Introductions*. New York: MacMillan Co., 1961.

...... *A Vision*. New York: Collier-MacMillan, 1966; London: MacMillan, 1956.